The McGraw-Hill Guide to

EFFECTIVE BUSINESS REPORTS

The McGraw-Hill Guide to

EFFECTIVE BUSINESS REPORTS

Roy W. Poe

McGRAW-HILL BOOK COMPANY

New York St. Louis San Francisco Auckland
Bogotá Hamburg Johannesburg London Madrid
Mexico Montreal New Delhi Panama Paris
São Paulo Singapore Sydney Tokyo Toronto

Library of Congress Cataloging in Publication Data
Poe, Roy W.
   The McGraw-Hill guide to effective business reports.

   Includes index.
   1.Business report writing.   I.Title.
HF5719.P63   808′.066651021   81-6062
ISBN 0-07-050341-9   AACR2

2 3 4 5 6 7 8 9 0 DODO 8 9 8 7 6 5 4 3 2

ISBN 0-07-050341-9

The editors for this book were William Sabin and Christine M. Ulwick, the designer was Mark E. Safran, and the production supervisor was Thomas G. Kowalczyk. It was set in Korinna by University Graphics, Inc.

Art and layout by Small Kaps Associates, Inc.

Contents

About this book

Let's try to draw a bead on you. You're in sales or marketing or accounting-data processing or public relations, personnel, finance, production-manufacturing, purchasing, systems, or general administration. And although everybody in the executive suite talks a lot about reducing paper communications ("My god, look at my desk!"), no one has made the first move to stem the flow. So you write a good number of reports or are aiming at a spot higher up in the organization where you're likely to.

If we have identified you correctly, this book is for you. You can find any number of tomes on report writing in libraries and bookstores. Probably you've even bought a couple, hoping to find just the right guide to help you produce reports that earn you consistent applause from your boss and others. Chances are, though, you were disappointed with your purchase. Not because the book wasn't any good—there are some fine ones—but because it focused on the kinds of reports you *don't* write. If you're not involved in research (market, scientific, new-product, engineering, etc.), you're not going to produce many reports that win high marks from graduate-school deans who concern themselves with purity in research and "objective" writing.

You can count on just a few fingers, report-writing books that zero in on such reports as these:

- There is trouble in the Customer Services Unit. Orders from customers are back-logged, employee turnover has risen sharply, and the general morale is bad. What's wrong, and what can be done about the situation? Somebody says: "Let's look hard at this situation and put our findings and solutions in a written report."

- Profits are down, and the president has issued a directive that says, in effect, "Cut every expense to the bone." This means a tentative moratorium on hiring, taking trips, lavish entertainment of customers, and so on. One department head, who urgently needs two new people, thinks he can persuade management to make an exception to this policy and decides that the idea can best be sold by means of a written report.

- Several department heads and supervisors are critical of the company's lack of attention to management development. They maintain that good executives are not born—they are developed through classroom and experience programs. The executive vice president, though, thinks that effective managers automatically rise to the top, without benefit of formal in-company educational programs. The people concerned decide to describe their needs and recommendations in writing.

- Your boss wonders why you are consistently over your expense budget—last month by 20 percent. You've had several conversations about it, but since the situation hasn't improved, you've been asked to defend your position in a brief memorandum.

And so on. Although the specific subjects described may not be pertinent to your job, the type of communication called for in each instance is typical of modern business reporting. Most are fairly short, written as memorandums, and somewhat informally worded and structured.

And that's the theme of this book. Although we cover a few longer, formally structured reports, we concentrate on the shorter, day-to-day communications. Emphasis is on organization, clear writing (word choice, sentence and paragraph structure, personal style, and structural correctness), logic, bias-free exposition, display (with special attention to numerical data), and "salesmanship."

As we introduce these principles of good writing, we involve you constantly. That is, throughout the book are exercises (called "Your Turn") that we hope you will want to tackle. They'll get you to edit other people's writing—that is, look for problems and fix them. They'll give you a chance to see whether you have understood the principles discussed and can apply them appropriately in the given situations. In "educationese," this is called *reinforcement,* and it's a great device for learning. (Suggested solutions to all the "Your Turn" exercises are in the back of the book.)

As you leaf through the book, you will see many examples of reports, each with an analysis, in a side-by-side arrangement. We hope you will take the time to read not only the reports themselves but the right-hand comments as well. With this device, along with the "Your Turn" exercises, we expect to make you an active participant in the learning process, not just a passive reader.

Once you get in the habit of looking critically at other people's material—spotting weaknesses and devising ways to overcome them—we think this habit will carry over to your own writing. The reports you used to send forward as "finished work" are now likely to appear to you as first-draft efforts that need the same kind of critical rereading and reworking that you'll be doing as you proceed through this book.

Maybe you'll even get the idea that writing good reports is, if not exactly fun, a creative experience that can provide a lot of satisfaction. Maybe open new doors for you.

ROY W. POE

PART 1

How to think about reports

Just about every written communication is a report. It might be as simple as a while-you-were-out telephone message or as complex as a 200-page analysis of marketing strategy. This is why it is almost impossible to define a business report. A ten-year study of personnel turnover, a one-page comparative income statement, a lavishly illustrated annual report to stockholders, and a memo suggesting new procedures for handling merchandise returns—all are reports.

Nor does it help much to try to put business reports into discrete categories, as many writers have done. They like to attach such labels as progress reports, information reports, analytical reports, investigative reports, research reports, and so on. The trouble here is that a single report may deserve all these labels. So let's dispense with a precise definition and say this: Any time you transmit facts, opinions, proposals, or recommendations, you are reporting.

It's no secret that in the typical organization the reports aren't very good. Many are downright awful. A casual sampling of a day's worth of written reports will reveal such shortcomings as:

- Hit-or-miss organization
- Overwriting
- Lack of purpose and direction
- Bias in expressing facts or opinions
- Fifty-dollar words and phrases that defy translation
- Pompous, stilted language and awkward construction

plus a dozen others. The purpose of this book is to help you avoid these pitfalls and learn how to write clear, intelligent, and persuasive reports.

Let's start off by looking at an excerpt from a personnel report. The writer is discussing the importance of classifying and describing each job when setting up a salary administration program.

The key to a successful salary administration program is the proper classification of all employees. The fruits of a careful job evaluation plan can be completely destroyed by a subsequent improper classification of employees. Extreme care must be exercised in ensuring that each employee is assigned the proper job classification. Arbitrary assignments to higher classifications to protect earnings or because of nepotism or supervisory favoritism must be avoided.

Following the installation of the program, successful salary control requires that the job classifications and job descriptions be constantly reviewed and brought up to date. Administrative procedures must be provided so that employees who detect changes in their job content may have the job description reviewed and, if necessary, reevaluated. Supervisors should be particularly alert for creeping changes—particularly true in office clerical jobs where new assignments are made from time to time which separately do not represent significant increase in job content but in total do represent added responsibility.

Study the excerpt carefully and see if you can pinpoint the writer's weaknesses. The following questions will guide you.

1. Is it interesting to read?
2. Are terms clearly defined and used consistently?
3. Do you find evidence of repetition?
4. Is the author's meaning always clear?
5. Is the author guilty of overwriting?

Now let's analyze the report together.

1. The report is dull. The writer has used stodgy expressions and awkward sentences. The passage has no life.
2. The terms are confusing. The writer has not sorted out for us the meaning of *classification, job evaluation plan, salary administration, salary control,* and *job description.* Some terms seem to be intended as synonyms for others, but we aren't sure.
3. There is a good deal of repetition. For example, the first three sentences say essentially the same thing.
4. Frequently, the meaning is not clear. In the fourth sentence, for example, the writer introduces several points that presumably illustrate his or her earlier premise, yet the ideas seem entirely negative and irrelevant. The last sentence in the report shows fuzzy thinking—it's hard to know what was intended.
5. The author is indeed guilty of overwriting—too many "garbage" words and nonsense sentences. These weaknesses are usually the result of the writer's not thinking through the report before beginning to write.

Many business reports read like rough drafts—that is, preliminary copy that needs thoughtful editing. If the writer had done some planning, including outlining the ideas in the copy to see if they are "outlinable," a much better report would have been produced. Let's look at an edited version.

An effective salary administration program depends largely on intelligent job classification, backed up by a complete description of each job. If the process of classifying and describing each job is haphazard, it will be impossible to establish meaningful and fair compensation levels.

Nor is job classification a one-time thing. Jobs change constantly, and we must review each one frequently to make sure that workers are actually doing what their job descriptions say they should be doing. Often employees (especially clerical workers) are given new responsibilities—tasks well beyond their job description—without additional compensation. A salary administration plan that does not recognize such changes can hardly ensure equal opportunities to employees. Some will be short-changed, others overpaid.

We think you'll agree that the revised copy is much better than the original. It is more interesting, easier to read, and clearer. Did you notice that the second version is a good deal shorter? You will nearly always produce a more readable report when you hone your material down to its basic elements.

In Chapter 1, which follows, we'll explore the what, who, why, when, and how of business reports.

CHAPTER 1

The what, who, why, when, and how of business reports

WHAT REPORTS ARE—AND ARE NOT

A lot of people think of a business report as a fat document that looks something like a scholarly dissertation, full of formal headings like *Objective, Method, Scope, Delineations,* and *Conclusions.* Certainly that's one kind of business report, and you ought to know how to put one together. But these "formal" reports aren't all that common in most jobs. Relatively few people write them. On the other hand, nearly everyone who has responsibilities for people, performance, and money writes a great many reports of another variety: the informal, often persuasive, report concerning everyday operational matters. For example:

- You're asked by your boss to justify, in writing, your reasons for exceeding your departmental expense budget by 20 percent in the first quarter.
- You have some ideas for streamlining a certain operation in the company that, if accepted, could result in big savings.
- The Operations Committee, of which you are a member, asks you to find out how the volume of merchandise returns in your company last year compares with that in several other similar organizations.
- One of your new subordinates does outstanding work and you want to reward her with a 15 percent salary increase even though, according to personnel policy, she's not due for an increase for at least six months.

"But those situations just require memos," you might say. True, many of them will be written in memorandum form. But memorandums are also reports. And dealing with even routine situations such as those described requires writing skill and, often, persuasiveness. This is why the emphasis in this book is on the everyday report—the kind you are most likely to write.

WHY WRITTEN REPORTS?

The primary job of a business report is to furnish information to one or more people who, on the basis of that information, can make a decision, form an opinion, or simply become enlightened. In larger organizations, it isn't possible for managers and executives to see everyone who has information to convey, and they must depend on written reports for that information. Distance, too, is a factor. If you work for a company that has several subsidiary offices throughout the country, you're well aware that the firm's operations can be coordinated only by written communications.

Written reports, then, solve the problems of size (in terms of number of employees) and distance. But there are other reasons why written reports have become indispensable to most organizations:

1. Reports often contain figures and other data that are very complex, and it would be impossible for the receiver to understand and remember the details when they are merely spoken about.

2. Information communicated orally requires immediate (and often hasty) attention. A written report, on the other hand, can be attended to at the convenience of the recipient; that is, it can be set aside and read later when it can be given concentrated attention.

3. Written reports provide information about the organization's past—its changing structure, personnel, policies, operations, and growth—information that may be highly valuable to management in making decisions about the future. More and more, information from reports finds its way into computers where it can be made available instantly to those who need it.

4. Hundreds of organizations have published histories of their enterprises, and every year there are additional ones. The company archives, consisting largely of reports, are a prime source for these histories.

WHO WRITES REPORTS?

Nearly everyone who has responsibilities for people, products, services, policies, operations, or money writes reports. In the typical large company, every supervisor, manager, and executive receives several reports daily and, at the same time, prepares reports for others to read.

Almost every executive you talk to complains about the amount of paperwork he or she must deal with. Yet these very same people are the first to admit that they can't make intelligent decisions without hard evidence—and hard evidence nearly always means a written document. So while top executives protest and vow to cut down on the volume of paperwork, they are constantly triggering additional reports. The reason is simple: *the need to know.*

It is highly likely, therefore, that writing reports of one kind or another will occupy a good chunk of your working day. If this is not true now, it surely will be as you move up the ladder. As long as your responsibilities for people or other assets are minimal, your reports are likely to be occasional, brief memos that contain facts you have been asked to supply. But when you start to climb, your paperwork activity accelerates rapidly. Ask any sales representative who has just been promoted to field supervisor or an accountant whose new title now includes "manager" or "director." When your responsibilities for people or money expand, your accountability increases, and this means supplying information in writing to your boss, your subordinates, and others about procedures, progress, policies, and many other important business matters.

A lot of people, before entering business, have the notion that all or most of their business writing will be letters to customers, suppliers, and others outside the organization. This is simply not so for the majority. The accounting manager, personnel relations director, systems supervisor, and materials handling specialist—to name just a few—will usually write ten or twenty in-house reports for every letter that goes outside.

WHEN TO WRITE REPORTS

When should you write a report? The obvious answer to that question would seem to be: when you're asked to do so by someone who outranks you. Some executives demand reports from their subordinates frequently. On the other hand, there are some who almost never do. But this should not stop you from writing on your own initiative: you need a bigger staff, or you want additional equipment, or you're not happy with the salary structure in your department, or you want certain personnel policies changed. Don't hesitate to put your thoughts on paper—that is, if you think you have a good chance of getting what you want.

Sometimes you're forced to write because you can't nail down your boss for a personal conference. Certain executives never seem to have time for a face-to-face meeting of any decent length. Or when they do grant an hour's appointment, they spend the time reading their mail or sorting desk papers while the "reporter" tries to get their attention. The only hope in these instances is to put your case in writing. A face-to-face presentation may be half-heard and quickly forgotten (or denied). But a written document commands attention; it is almost impossible for the receiver *not* to read it and make some sort of intelligent response.

Still, you have to use judgment. Some people write too often and too much, flooding the desks of their superiors with communications that concern the most routine matters that could have easily been handled by a telephone call or a chance meeting in the hallway. Possibly these "overwriters" think that a written report always scores points. Not so. A situation that calls for weighing heady alternatives and possibly spending a good deal of money—such as a sweeping organizational change—does deserve a written report. A decision that you're supposed to make—such as staggering the hours of three of your clerical people—usually does not. Your boss's attitude toward paper communications should certainly influence your output. If your boss shudders at the sight of "more paperwork," you will certainly be highly selective about what you put in writing.

PROTOCOL IN BUSINESS REPORTS

When you write a report to a superior—whether on demand or self-initiated—only that person is usually entitled to see it. Unless instructed otherwise, don't send copies to other people. One executive we know wrote a detailed memo to the vice president, recommending a big promotion and salary increase for Ms. X, revealing information about the salaries and performance of a number of Ms. X's associates in the department. A copy was sent to Ms. X and was so indicated on the original. The result: no salary increase or promotion for Ms. X and a rather resounding warning to her boss.

Sometimes your boss's superior asks for a report on an important matter, and your boss turns the assignment over to you. Unless otherwise told, address the report to your boss. He can then "cover" it with a memo and send it on, or if he prefers, he can draw on it in composing a memo he sends forward in his own name.

It may be that your boss will want you to write such a report in your own name and address it to the higher-up executive who requested it. When this is done, be sure to indicate that your boss is receiving a copy. In the first place, you want your boss to know what's in your report; in the second place, you want to be sure no one gets the idea you've exceeded your authority.

When you plan to write a report to anyone who is not your own subordinate, be safe and "copy" the boss. And when you are thinking about writing to an executive outside your own department—especially one on the same level or a higher level than your boss—make sure your superior knows your intention beforehand and, when the report is done, gets a copy. Insensitivity to these delicate aspects of corporate politics could bring you unnecessary grief.

REPORTS AND YOUR FUTURE

It is not uncommon for newcomers to win their first recognition on the basis of the reports they write. Indeed, the principal contact you have with top management for many months after your arrival may be a "paper connection." And top management is quick to spot competence in written communications. These executives see many reports that are badly organized, poorly constructed, faulty in logic, biased, and hard to understand. Thus, a really good report stands out. We can't think of a better reason for learning how to write good reports.

Obviously, the best report writers are not automatically the best executives. Nor is it necessarily true that, say, accountants who can't write well are poor accountants. But good executives are much better ones if they *can* write. Those with clout in the organization constantly evaluate middle management people for their potential, and often the only available yardstick is their written communication.

So it all boils down to this: No matter how expert you are in your field of specialization, you may be denied your potential niche in higher management if you lack the ability to write clear, accurate, and convincing reports. It's worth pushing yourself a bit to develop this skill. The rewards will surely justify the effort.

THREE BASIC GUIDELINES

In thinking about writing good reports, you will want to observe these three basic guidelines:

1. Know who your reader is.
2. Have a clear purpose.
3. Define your perimeters.

Know Who Your Reader Is

Before you tackle a report-writing assignment, you should have a clear idea of who will read it. This sounds elementary; yet it is surprising how many reports read as though they were written to whom-it-may-concern. The reader (or readers) of your report will determine, to a large extent, your language and writing style, depth of coverage, emphasis, terminology, and format. So the reader is everything.

Language and Style. There is a good deal of disagreement about what is and is not appropriate language and style in business reports. One report-writing book defines a report as "an objective, impartial presentation of facts." Unfortunately, the definition is wrong. In many reports, you may have few if any facts to draw from; for example, what the company's sales volume is likely to be ten years hence. Here, opinion—based largely on conjecture—is wanted. Or you may have a good supply of facts, such as sheaves of financial statements which clearly prove that the rate of return on investments has been slipping steadily for the past three years. What we need to know is *why,* and each person who analyzes the problem may come up with entirely different reasons.

Even more bothersome in the definition given is the word *objective,* which really means bending over backwards to keep the language impersonal. Compare:

FORMAL, IMPERSONAL	CONVERSATIONAL
Unexpectedly, the first Open House drew over 2000 people, a positive indication that such an endeavor is worthwhile in terms of community relations.	We were surprised and delighted to have over 2000 visitors at our first Open House. Surely this is proof that the community is interested in what we are doing.

It is true that some reports are weighty in tone, with the somewhat somber language you see in the example at the left. Such reports are likely to concern matters of great importance, such as a proposal for a revision of the company pension plan, or an objective comparison of two proposed locations for a new distribution center, or the results of a brand-recognition study. In these instances, the subject as well as the reader determines language and style. A brief report to the boss on the success of the company's first Open House, however, would seem to call for a style that is more conversational than formal. This is why we would choose the example at the right as more fitting in this particular instance.

Guides for Determining Writing Style. Although we can't tell you whether your writing style should be formal or conversational, we can offer a couple of generalizations:

1. Reports that travel upward—to the higher rungs of management—tend to be a little more formal than those that travel laterally or downward.

2. Reports about critical matters that could have a heavy impact on company policy or procedure will be somewhat more serious in tone than those concerning more-or-less routine matters. For example, a report to your boss in which you seek permission to reorganize your department is likely to be a good deal more conversational than one proposing renting warehouse space instead of constructing a new building.

It is our experience that in typical reports in which you are making suggestions, proposals, or recommendations concerning fairly routine matters, most readers prefer a human touch. Not chatty, flip, or cute, to be sure, but natural—much as you would word a letter to a valuable customer whom you consider a personal friend.

Still, even when your style is impersonal, there is no reason to be stuffy. If you *have* to be impersonal, you can still write clearly, understandably, even interestingly. Compare:

IMPERSONAL BUT CLEAR

It appears that the best compensation plan is one that offers both security and incentive. Talks with several sales representatives revealed a serious concern about the straight commission plan. Even though they are aware of the possibility of making more money under this plan, it is not attractive. They would rather be assured of a monthly income they know they can count on.

IMPERSONAL AND STUFFY

The most equitable arrangement is undoubtedly one which results in both security and incentive. This truism was demonstrated repeatedly in confrontations with numerous sales representatives in which there were constant expressions of great trepidation toward the so-called straight commission arrangement. Albeit, there is awareness of potentially greater earnings, the uncertainty of a sufficient income to dispose of obligations makes the latter arrangement unfeasible.

On the other hand, if your reader (and the subject) permits a conversational style, you can make your reports a lot more interesting. For example:

I believe the best compensation plan is one that offers both security and incentive. The sales representatives I talked with are suspicious of a straight commission deal. Although they know they might make more money under this plan, the lack of a fixed income is a real worry.

Reader Bias. Try to find out whether your reader has personal biases that you have to keep in mind when you write your report. Some executives, for example, welcome innovations, while others are slow to accept change. Let's say you think certain operations for which you are responsible should be computerized, which will cost a lot of money at the outset but eventually save a great deal. If you know that the person who receives your report has been known to refer to computers as expensive playthings, your report should state specifically how much can be saved and over what time period, with a lot of supporting evidence. Or let's say that the person you want to sell an idea to is proud of his or her reputation as an expert with figures and being hard-nosed when it comes to spending money. Knowing this particular trait, you're not likely to emphasize beauty or decor when you recommend the expenditure of $4500 for new office furniture. Instead, concentrate on such factors as increased efficiency, greater production, improved morale, and the like.

Familiarity with Subject Matter. Another reason it's important to pinpoint your reader at the outset is that you must know how much he or she knows about the situation that prompted you to write a report. The organization of your report, the general content, and the choice of words will depend largely on the reader's familiarity with the subject. You do not want to launch into the solution of a certain problem when you have no evidence that your reader is aware that there *is* a problem. A report to your boss about a situation that the two of you have already discussed requires little, if any, background information. But if you know that the report is likely to be read by others who are not in on the problem, you will have to put the issue in its proper perspective before proceeding with the main points of your report.

As to the language you use, remember that every area of business has its own special jargon. When you're writing to people outside your particular specialty, you must make sure you don't use words they're not likely to be familiar with. For example, the chief budget officer who issues instructions to all managers and supervisors on budget preparation may have to define such terms as ROI, medium-range forecast, and accruals and deferrals. If these instructions were going only to the accounting staff, such terms would be readily understood.

The Reader-Writer Relationship. If your reader is a personal friend and you don't have to worry about rank or position, you can take certain liberties with language and style that you would not take if the reader is a top executive and lets no one forget it. Although the latter might not object to a conversational style—indeed may prefer it—you're wise to guard your language.

Your position in the company can also have a bearing on the way you express yourself. If you are an expert in a certain area, say, group insurance programs or space planning or employee training, you can speak with some authority in that area and be somewhat assertive in making recommendations. But if you write on a subject that is well outside your specialization and about which you are presumed to be something less than an expert, your recommendations in a report, if any, should be made cautiously. Here is an example. The subject is personnel training.

WRITER HAS VIRTUALLY NO EXPERIENCE IN PERSONNEL TRAINING

It seems unlikely that Fairchild has the staff needed to handle all education and training that employees need. And to obtain the number required would be very expensive. Is it possible that we could find sources of training outside the company—say, in local colleges and universities?

WRITER IS THOROUGHLY EXPERIENCED IN PERSONNEL TRAINING

No companies that I know of are in a position to do all the education and training of employees. It's too big a job and very expensive. Based on my experience in other companies, the best solution is to arrange with local colleges and universities to provide much of the training—certainly in the academic subjects. Usually, these institutions are eager to cooperate and often offer special tuition plans.

Have a Clear Purpose

Every report must have a purpose. We emphasize this seemingly obvious fact because all too often writers don't bother to state what their purpose is. And the message often has little meaning or impact when the reader is left to grapple with the question, Why did I get this document?

Granted, the purpose of many routine reports is understood without the writer's having to state it, such as financial statements that are circulated monthly, periodic production reports, and annual personnel turnover reports. Such reports are usually prepared at the direction of top managers and executives, and everyone who gets them knows their purpose and the use that is to be made of them.

On the other hand, most narrative reports (those that rely primarily on words rather than figures) require either a statement of purpose or a reference that identifies purpose. In informal memorandums, reference to a previous request or a conversation serves as the statement of purpose. For example:

1. Attached is my report on our direct-mail activities for the first quarter, which you telephoned me about last Thursday.

2. At the May meeting of the Operations Committee, there was a good deal of discussion about the increasing problem of warehouse pilferage. I have some ideas that I think may help to reduce these losses.

3. You asked for my reactions to J. O. Grady's recommendation that the company centralize all contract files in the treasurer's office. In this brief report I will outline the pros and cons of this suggestion as viewed by the members of the Purchasing Section.

4. When the subject of bonuses came up at the Sales Managers Committee meeting in July, I was on the side of those who saw no compelling reason to change our present compensation plan. After an extensive field study, however, I have some new thoughts on the matter and I want to share them with you.

5. Here is the revised budget for the Order Services Department (requested in your memo of May 11), along with my comments on the probable effect on our operation of a proposed 20 percent overhead reduction.

In longer reports that deal with more complex matters, the purpose is usually specifically stated, including the background information needed by the reader to understand why the report was written.

PURPOSE

A recent study of retail stores in Greater Wilmington reveals that Unger's is the only major store in the area that accepts no credit cards except its own. All the others offer bank-card credit privileges.

What effect has our policy had on sales volume in the past two years? What is likely to happen to sales and profits if we change our policy? The purpose of this report is to examine this controversial subject and to suggest guidelines for future policy.

Knowing What Is Wanted.   When you originate a report, your purpose ought to be easy to identify. You know what you want to accomplish. However, when you are directed by a superior to prepare a report, the purpose may be somewhat vague in your mind because the instructions may have been given "on the run." It is not unusual to receive a telephone request something like this: "Let me have a complete analysis of our direct-mail activities for the third quarter." In your haste to be agreeable, you might say, "Fine—right away." But as you sit down to plan your report and gather the data for it, you realize that you really don't know what is wanted. What kind of analysis? Cost only? Effectiveness in terms of responses received? Results in comparison with other media? Types of direct-mail pieces used? All of these?

When you are asked for a report, then, always make certain that you and the requester are on the same wavelength. Although you may prefer to guess rather than to appear dense, you will be doing no one a favor (especially yourself) by delivering a communication that misses the mark. To save everybody's time, jot down what you *think* is wanted; then quickly confirm it with the person who asked for the report.

Define Your Perimeters

Sometimes it is necessary to tell your reader what your report does *not* cover as well as what it does. For example, assume that you have been asked to make a study of the use of employment tests in various companies in your industry. You decide to concentrate on two of the major types of tests—mental ability and psychological—but not to deal with a third major type, the job performance test. Early in your report you will want to make specific reference to your elimination of performance tests. This will alert readers, some of whom may be test experts, to the fact that the omission was intentional and not the result of ignorance.

Establishing boundaries for your discussion is often important, too. If you do not do so, your reader may make assumptions that are not valid. For example:

> Here is the report you asked for on our stock control system. It contains a number of suggestions that I believe will result in better inventory management and possible reduction in personnel.
>
> In my report, I have assumed that the present system will be maintained. Although I think the ultimate answer to our inventory management problem is to put the entire system on the computer, I realize that this possibility has already been ruled out for this year.

One Major Subject Per Report. Speaking of perimeters, you should limit each report to one major subject. For example, if your purpose is to analyze the weaknesses in the company's cash control system and make recommendations for change, you probably would not discuss in the same report the need to set up new equipment records or a different method of handling merchandise returns. These latter two topics are best covered in separate reports. Bootlegging them into your cash control report will weaken its impact, and the two additional topics won't get the attention they deserve.

MAKING REPORTS READABLE

Once you identify your reader, understand clearly the purpose of your report, and define your perimeters, you are ready to think about putting the report together so that the message you want to get across comes across. This means:

- Using the right words
- Writing effective sentences and paragraphs
- Writing so that people believe you
- Selling your ideas
- Writing with appropriate emphasis
- Displaying your message effectively

In the chapters that follow, we'll show you how to do the six things listed.

HIGHLIGHTS OF CHAPTER 1

1. Reports are submitted in writing because written reports:

   a. Solve communication problems that arise out of size (personnel) and distance.

   b. Make it easier for the receiver to understand and remember complicated data.

   c. Permit concentrated attention of readers at their leisure.

   d. Provide information about the organization's changing structure, personnel, policies, operations, and growth—information which aids in making current decisions.

   e. Become repositories for company histories.

2. The higher that people rise in an organization, the more likely they are to write business reports.

3. Three basic rules about when you should write reports are:

   a. You should write reports, of course, when you are directed by someone of higher rank to do so.

   b. You should write reports on your own initiative when you want to share valuable information with others or simply sell an idea or a point of view.

   c. You should avoid writing reports when the information could just as easily and effectively be presented orally.

4. Three important rules to remember about protocol in business reports are:

   a. When you write to a superior, do not send copies to anyone else unless instructed to do so.

   b. When you are asked by your boss to write a report in your own name to his or her superior, indicate that your boss is receiving a copy.

   c. When you write a report to people in the organization who are not your subordinates, send a copy to the boss.

5. It is important to know who your reader is for the following reasons:

   a. The language and style are often determined by the preferences of the person who is to read the report. Generally, reports to higher echelons are a little more formal than those that travel laterally or downward.

   b. Your reader may have biases that have to be taken into account.

   c. Familiarity with the subject is likely to vary from reader to reader.

6. Every report should have a clear purpose. In some financial and production reports, the purpose is understood and need not be stated. In most narrative reports, however, the specific reason for writing the report must be stated or strongly implied.

7. Sometimes it is necessary to define the perimeters of your report—that is, tell the reader what the report does not cover as well as what it does.

8. Each report should be limited to one major subject.

Informal reports

If you're like most people, the reports you write—at least at the outset—will be of the simple, everyday type. The following are typical situations:

1. Your boss, the director of marketing, has asked for suggestions from the staff for ways of providing incentives to sales representatives to encourage them to do a better job of selling and, at the same time, advance in their career with the company. You decide to suggest a new compensation plan whereby sales representatives can earn commissions and bonuses based on individual performance.

2. The personnel director isn't happy with the employee orientation program the company now operates and thinks a big change is desirable. You are asked to analyze the weaknesses of the present program and make your recommendations for change.

3. The company you work for is having a hard time holding on to its sales representatives in the New England region. There have been several defections to competitors, and the company is becoming alarmed. You are asked to make a visit to the region and, based on what you find out, submit your recommendations for action.

4. The workload in your department has expanded dramatically, and you find that you can't do your job unless you hire an additional person. But because sales are soft and expenses are over budget, the company has set a no-new-hiring policy until the profit picture improves. You think your situation is so desperate that an exception should be made.

THE MEMORANDUM AS A REPORT

The memorandum is by far the most popular format for everyday reports since its printed headings made it easy to identify the recipient, the writer, and the subject. And it is self-transmitting; that is, you don't have to cover it with a separate document.

In the four situations described earlier, the reports are likely to be written as interoffice memorandums. Memo formats differ, but the following is typical.

Killiam-Butler Corporation

Interoffice
Memorandum

To: Mr. John C. Fenimore

Subject: Promotion-From-Within Policy

From: K. T. Pogue

Date: February 2, 19--

Some memo headings are more detailed. Depending on the size of the company, the heading may also include department title, location, and telephone number for both the recipient and the writer, as well as other information.

CHAPTER 2

Using the right words

Assume you have been asked by the marketing director for suggestions on ways of providing incentives to salespeople to encourage them to do a better job and, at the same time, advance in their career with the company. You feel that sales representatives should be given not only a regular salary but commissions and bonuses as well, the amount to be based on individual performance. This is the theme of your report.

Since your report will be addressed to your boss and the subject is not especially complicated or weighty, you will probably choose a writing style that is informal, personal. The boss will receive perhaps a dozen or so other suggestions, and you want yours to stand out.

Suppose *you* are the marketing director and receive a report that started off like this:

Killiam-Butler Corporation

Interoffice Memorandum

To: Mr. Kevin C. Riesling   From: G. L. Gorham

Subject: Incentives for Sales Representatives   Date: July 17, 19--

Commensurate with overall plans to upgrade sales personnel and provide more viable opportunities for advancement, it is suggested that a revision of the existing compensatory plan be effectuated with a view toward tangible recognition of personal and individual performance. This is the thrust of the presentation which follows.

IMPORTANCE OF WORD USAGE

"Write reports so that I can read them quickly and with complete understanding" is a constant plea of management. Alas, the writer of the paragraph above paid no attention to the plea. You probably think there is really no excuse for using such language (some people call it "gobbledygook"), and you are right. Yet gobbledygook is the trademark of untold numbers of business and government writers.

It is tempting, to be sure, to select showy words: the importance of a wide vocabulary has been drilled into us since we started school. But a business report is not the place to display a flair for such terms as *commensurate with, viable opportunities, be effectuated, tangible recognition,* and *thrust.* Executives who have to read dozens of similar passages every day are to be pitied. No wonder they constantly shout at their subordinates, "Keep it simple!"

BUSINESSESE AND FEDERALESE

During the past several years, a style of writing has emerged in business and government that bewildered readers have labeled *businessese* and *federalese.* Businessese and federalese can easily be recognized, for they are styles that are labored, pompous, and abstruse ("abstruse" is a businessese word that means *hard to understand*). The language in the previous memo is a good example.

Look at the five examples of businessese/federalese writing at the left and compare them with the plain English version at the right.

BUSINESSESE/FEDERALESE

1. A well-conceived organization constitutes a fundamental component of efficacious office management.

2. The key to effective idea stimulation from employees lies in a good communication effort encompassing various media, including bulletin boards and the company periodical.

3. Stuffiness in a room tends toward drowsiness, as does a high temperature.

4. The task of inventorying the company records can be greatly simplified by the utilization of a form on which can be listed description, location, function, and department using records.

5. At the time of the development of the standard specifications for office forms, consideration is mandatory of the actual uses of a particular form in the office operational system.

PLAIN ENGLISH

1. Good office management can come about only if there is the right kind of organization.

2. If you want employees to offer ideas, it is important that you publicize their contributions—for example, in the company newspaper and on bulletin boards.

3. People get drowsy in a room that is overheated or lacks fresh air.

4. The forms inventory will be easier if you use a sheet with these headings: Description, Location, Function, and Department.

5. When you set up standard specifications for office forms, be sure to keep in mind how each form will actually be used.

It is obvious that the "plain English" examples are much easier to read and understand. In some cases, this is because we have used personal references (2, 4, and 5), which nearly always lighten up dark passages. Even so, you can still write simply and clearly without personal references. Compare:

FEDERALESE

Many government offices have experienced difficulty in hiring personnel for messenger service. The classification of messenger has been necessarily evaluated at a relatively low compensation level and is, ergo, unattractive to permanent employees. Furthermore, a positive self-image is lacking.

PLAIN ENGLISH

The job of messenger is hard to fill in many government offices. The salary is low, and the employee has no pride in the work. So even those who accept the job don't stay long.

YOUR TURN

Rewrite the following "businessese" sentence so that it is easier to understand; then check your rewrite with the one on page 190. You may use either a conversational style or an impersonal style.

It is imperative that careful attention be given to the selection of a particular machine so that the selection process results in the choice of a machine best suited for the job to be accomplished.

Another annoying habit of business and government writers is deliberately choosing "wise" and "ize" words—*businesswise, profitwise, moneywise, policywise, personnelwise, optimize, maximize, finalize, circularize,* and even *definitize.*

Profitwise, the company would be in a better position if an attempt were made to *maximize* the utilization of mechanical equipment in order to *optimize* on the greatest economies.

COMPARE:

The company will earn a bigger profit if mechanical equipment is used wherever possible to keep costs down.

"Wise" and "ize" words are coined, of course, to save words—for example, *definitize* for *make final.* Although a word is saved, it is at the expense of clarity and simplicity. Rarely is one long word of several syllables a "saving" over two or three simple words.

Two favorites of some business writers are *effectuate* and *actuate.* Instead of writing, "The new policy will go into effect December 15," they say, "The new policy will be *effectuated* (or *actuated*) December 15."

YOUR TURN

See if you can "decode" the following sentences from business reports, rewriting them so that they are more easily understood. Suggested revisions are on page 190.

1. Given our limited capital situation, it is mandatory that the company prioritize its investments profitwise.
2. All travel expenses must be legitimized.
3. Weatherwise, the prospect of an outdoor program looks bleak.
4. Can the new policy be actuated by March 1?
5. Costwise, the best method of replicating the newsletter is the spirit duplicator.

CHOOSING THE SIMPLE WORD

In the preceding examples, you saw a number of words that, although not necessarily in the businessese or federalese category, are somewhat showy—*constitutes* for *makes up, component* for *part, specify* for *tell, utilization* for *use, mandatory* for *needed* or *required,* and so on. You will make your reports much easier to read and understand if you choose the simple, everyday word over the unfamiliar word of three or four syllables. Granted, there is often no good substitute for a long word. For example, if you are reporting on the earnings of employees, you will probably choose the term *compensation* rather than *pay,* since compensation is not so restrictive in meaning. And there are no really satisfactory synonyms for such terms as *specifications, characteristics, mechanization, juxtaposition, synergistic,* etc. Then, too, the terms of a particular profession have no meaningful substitutes: *annuity* (insurance), *amortization* (accounting), *marginal utility* (economics), *subsidiary* (management), *demand fluctuations* (marketing), *wage differentials* (personnel), and *linear programming* (manufacturing). But there are dozens of other terms for which you can find a simple substitute. Here are a few.

SHOWY	SIMPLER
cogitate	think about
cognizant	aware of
comprehend	see, understand
comprised	made up of
conjecture	think, believe
consummate	wind up, agree to
corroborate	confirm
deliberate upon	think about

disburse	pay
increment	increase, raise
initial	first
maximum results	best results
nominal	small, little
obviate	make unnecessary, prevent
originate	start, begin
proclivity	leaning
ratify	approve, confirm
rationale	basis, reason
remunerate	pay
scrutinize	examine, inspect, look at
transpire	happen
ultimate	final

Your Turn

Rewrite the following using simple, everyday words. Compare your version with the one on page 190.

The initial objective, therefore, is to maximize productivity and minimize expenditures. Provided that management is perspicacious, the outcome, profitwise, should be favorable and produce no deleterious morale effects personnelwise.

It isn't always the shorter word that is more familiar. For example, more people understand the word *beneficial* than the word *salutary,* the word *negligent* is more common than the word *derelict,* and *think* is usually a better word than *deem.* Notice that sometimes two or three simple words are needed to take the place of one showy word. But there is nothing wrong with that; your aim is to make your writing easy to read—not to save space on the page.

CLUTTER WORDS

"Clutter" words are those that simply take up space but add nothing to meaning. For example, the sentence *The color of the worksheets is "eye-ease" green* contains three clutter words: *The color of.* Better: *The worksheets are "eye-ease" green.*

The following statement contains a number of clutter words:

> The reason the sales discounts amount is so high this year is due to the fact that we have followed the policy of allowing cash discounts to customers who are not entitled to them.

Can you spot the clutter words? Here they are:

The reason the	(omit)
amount	(omit)
due to the fact that	(because)
followed the policy of	(omit)

The statement should therefore appear as follows:

> Sales discounts are high this year because we allowed cash discounts to customers who were not entitled to them.

To eliminate clutter expressions, edit your writing carefully. Your purpose is not necessarily to achieve brevity; it is to help your readers by removing deadwood that they have to hurdle over. Here are other examples.

CLUTTER EXPRESSIONS	EDITED
We take the position that **or** It is our opinion that	We believe that
A substantial majority of employees	Most employees
We held a meeting for the purpose of	We met to
During the course of our conversation	In our conversation
At this point in time	Today
In the event that we find ourselves in disagreement	If we disagree
In view of the fact that there is no significant difference in	Since there is no significant difference in
This policy has been in full force and effect for the period of a year	This policy has been in effect for a year
The trouble with the new form is that it was improperly designed in the first place	First, the new form was improperly designed
At a later date	Later

We limited our discussion to the basic essentials	We discussed only the essentials
In this connection, the writer would like to point out the discrepancy that exists between	Please note the discrepancy between
She is a person who does an excellent job as a programmer	She is an excellent programmer
The main consideration is a matter of time	The main consideration is time
Please plan in advance to present your recommendations when the next meeting is held	Please plan to present your recommendations at the next meeting
We seldom ever have occasion to ask employees to work overtime on Sunday	We seldom ask employees to work on Sunday

As you may have noticed, clutter words are often redundancies—that is, two terms that mean the same thing. Look at these:

REDUNDANT	CORRECT
attached hereto	attached
loan obligation	loan *or* obligation
budget forecast	budget *or* forecast
dollar amounts	dollars *or* amounts
massively large	massive
prompt and speedy	prompt *or* speedy
true facts	facts
vitally essential	vital *or* essential
8:30 a.m. in the morning	8:30 a.m.
assemble together	assemble
free gratis	free *or* gratis
and etc.	etc.
consensus of opinion	consensus
endorse on the back	endorse
follows after	follows
repeat again	repeat
revert back	revert
new beginner	beginner

YOUR TURN

The following sentences contain clutter words. Rewrite them, not only to remove the deadwood and redundancies but to make these sentences easy to understand. Compare your revisions with those on page 190.

1. Attached hereto is the report on fleet truck rentals per your request under date of April 17.

2. We are in receipt of Ramco's bid for construction of the distribution center to be located in Modesto.

3. It is requested that you submit any and all recommendations at your earliest convenience.

4. If this proposal meets with your approval, kindly sign in the space provided on the line below.

5. The writer would like to take this opportunity to express special appreciation for the cooperation received from various and sundry staff members in the Personnel Department.

6. The Salary Review Committee will meet Tuesday morning at 10:00 o'clock a.m.

7. I want to reiterate again the importance of speed in attacking this problem so that it can be solved as soon as feasibly possible.

8. Please staple the pages together so that there is minimum danger of their being lost or misplaced.

NON SEQUITURS

Although it is important that you edit your writing to get rid of deadwood and redundancies, it is equally important that you not omit any vital material. Beware of the *non sequitur* (a Latin term for "it does not follow")—that is, omitting so many steps in your presentation that the reader cannot understand the connection between statements. For example:

NON SEQUITUR

The Clarksville Distribution Center has now been completed, and we have contracted with City Transportation Company for bus service.

CLEAR

The Clarksville Distribution Center has now been completed. Since there is no public transportation serving that area, many people have no means of getting to and from work. We have therefore contracted with City Transportation Company for bus service.

NON SEQUITUR

We have had a great deal of difficulty finding a sufficient number of secretaries for our needs and are establishing secretarial training programs.

CLEAR

We have had a great deal of difficulty finding a sufficient number of secretaries for our needs, and have reached the conclusion that the only answer to the problem is to train our own. We are therefore establishing secretarial training programs to which we hope to attract clerks, receptionists, and others who aspire to secretarial positions.

YOUR TURN

Now let's see how you would write the opening paragraph of the memo on page 17. Compare your rewrite with the one on page 191.

HIGHLIGHTS OF CHAPTER 2

1. Edit your writing to remove businessese and federalese.

   Checkup. Rewrite the following, avoiding pompous language. (See page 191 for a suggested rewrite.)

   In quality analysis and improvement, primary emphasis should be focused on long-range prevention of errors, rather than devoted merely to detection and correction.

2. Don't coin new words just to save space.

   Checkup. See if you can convey the same meaning in the sentence below without using "wise," "uate," and "ize" words. (See page 191 for a suggested rewrite.)

   Industrywise, it would appear to be unfeasible to effectuate new manufacturing standards until the results of the research have been maximized.

3. Choose simple, everyday words over showy words.

   Checkup. Rewrite the following, substituting simple words where appropriate. (See page 191 for a suggested rewrite.)

   A secondary method of reducing noise generation is the installation of partially muted telephonic bells in rooms containing a significant number of heavily utilized instruments.

4. Remove "deadwood" (unnecessary words) from your writing.

   Checkup. See if you can state the following in 20 words or less. (See page 191 for a suggested rewrite.)

   It is imperative that the factory supervisor exercise the best possible judgment in the censuring of workers as well as in acknowledging their favorable actions. This means, essentially, reprimanding recalcitrant workers in the privacy of the office and acknowledging the accomplishments of effective workers in a public atmosphere.

5. Avoid redundancies.

   Checkup. Edit the following for redundancies; then rewrite. (See page 191 for a suggested rewrite.)

   It is critically important to remember when designing and setting up an organization chart that it should reveal clearly and without question the reporting lines to each individual employee.

6. Watch out for non sequiturs.

   Checkup. See if you can supply the material that is missing in the following. (See page 191 for a suggested rewrite.)

   Tabulating the expected 200,000+ responses to the questionnaire will mean using the facilities of a time-sharing computer installation.

CHAPTER 3

Writing effective sentences and paragraphs

The right words will go a long way toward making your reports easy to read and understand. But words make up sentences, and sentences make up paragraphs. So you have to be a master at sentence and paragraph structure, too, if your reports are going to be really effective.

Let's take an example. Worldwide Distributors hires an average of twenty people a month. At present, the process of orienting these new employees is haphazard. The workers are simply given a brief welcome by someone on the personnel staff, handed a copy of the company's employee manual, and escorted to the departments where they will work.

The company personnel director is not satisfied with this procedure. She believes a formal induction program should be set up so that new employees get an in-depth exposure to the company. She asks an assistant for a recommendation on how a more effective program might be devised.

A section of the report submitted to the personnel director follows.

PRESENT PROCEDURE AND NEED FOR CHANGE

As you know, our present procedure for inducting new employees is brief and highly informal, one of us in Personnel giving employees a quick welcome, handing them a copy of "Worldwide's World," and escorting them to the departments where they will work—so there is really no program. With the rapid growth of the company, it becomes more and more difficult for employees to learn about our various products, the markets we serve, the firm's objectives and future plans, and who we are and what we do, so there is no opportunity for new employees to meet top executives, learn about interdepartmental relationships, and find out how their own department fits into the total picture, plus the matter of educating employees about such things as compensation, retirement, fringe benefits, and general company policies, all of which are important not only in avoiding costly errors but also from the standpoint of general morale, meaning the sense of belonging and pride in being a part of the organization.

The writer's choice of words and general writing style are fine. As you probably noticed, however, the sentences are too long and need to be broken up into individual thought units. Also, the copy is solid—that is, there are no "visual breaks" for the reader. The absence of good breaks makes any report hard to read, no matter how simple the words or ideas. So we need intelligent paragraphing, too, not only to provide "white space" but to separate one major idea from another.

SENTENCES

Sentences are the basic thought units of writing. Their length and general structure deserve just as much attention as the words you use.

Sentence Length

Many writers—probably most—tend to ignore sentence length as a factor in readability. Yet every study of readability clearly shows that readers have difficulty with long sentences. Unfortunately, it is not uncommon to find sentences in business and government reports that are 100 words or more in length. Even a *few* of these can ruin an otherwise effective communication.

What is the best sentence length? There is no definitive answer to that question. We can say, however, that when you begin to exceed eighteen to twenty words in a sentence, you should think about stopping. Beyond twenty words or so, a sentence begins to fall in the "difficult" category. This doesn't mean that there won't be some sentences in your report that are well beyond that number; sometimes you can't avoid them. But usually you can.

You may infer from this advice that all your sentences should be short. But this is not the case. Too many short sentences can make your report as hard to read as too many long ones. For example:

> Going public will permit us to raise additional equity capital. This should encourage a rapid growth of the company. Additional equity capital would also expand our credit base.

The paragraph above is choppy. Notice how much easier it is to follow when the statements are connected.

> Going public will permit us to raise additional equity capital, which should encourage a rapid growth of the company. Additional capital would also expand our credit base.

In terms of sentence length, the objective is to strive for *variety*—that is, a good mixture of both short and medium-length sentences. For example:

> General magazines with large, national distribution are not usually interested in company news. However, publications that serve special interests—women's fashions and home improvements, for example—are excellent media for product reports. Here we have to establish the right contact. What is the right contact? It is . . .

The reason that we see so many long sentences in reports is that the writer put two, three, or more ideas in the sentence. For example:

> The minimum essentials of a report to stockholders are a balance sheet, a statement of income and surplus, and an auditor's certification, and beyond these essentials the content of the report becomes an interesting challenge to corporate

imagination. The elements selected for the report, the order in which they appear, and the way they are presented are strictly up to management, but most reports will contain these elements: cover, title page, table of contents, company directory, financial highlights, and president's letter.

You can easily see that the two sentences above contain four distinct ideas. Let's separate them:

The minimum essentials of a report to stockholders are a balance sheet, a statement of income and surplus, and an auditor's certification. Beyond these essentials, the content of the report becomes an interesting challenge to corporate imagination. The elements selected for the report, the order in which they appear, and the way they are presented are strictly up to management. However, most reports will contain these elements: cover, title page, table of contents, company directory, financial highlights, and president's letter.

Your Turn

Break down the following passage into manageable thought units and edit out pompous words and labored writing. (See page 191 for a suggested rewrite.)

There are two overwhelming reasons for retaining records: for reference on the part of the company and to answer requests for information from the government, banks, and other institutions, but they also serve as a history of the company and act as a training medium for executive nominees. Therefore they should be retained covering all departments in the enterprise.

Tying Sentences Together

When you write a report, visualize yourself as taking readers by the hand and leading them through territory they are not familiar with. One help you can provide is a bridge that connects one idea with another.

It would be a mistake, in my opinion, to ignore these complaints from customers. We should not push the "panic button" every time we receive an irate letter.

As you can see, there is no bridge between the first and second sentences. Thus, the reader is led to believe that the second idea adds emphasis to the first. But it doesn't. Indeed, the second sentence is an entirely different thought. Let's put a bridge between them:

It would be a mistake, in my opinion, to ignore these complaints from customers. *On the other hand,* we should not push the "panic button" every time we receive an irate letter.

The bridge is, of course, *On the other hand.* This phrase prepares the reader for an abrupt shift in thought. Words and phrases that provide a bridge between sentences and between paragraphs are called transitional expressions. The following are examples.

TO SHOW CAUSE AND EFFECT

accordingly, for this reason, as a result, hence, therefore

Only three people signed up for the course in home repairs. *Therefore,* the course was canceled.

TO SHOW EXCEPTIONS OR CONTRAST

but, conversely, even though, however, on the contrary, on the other hand, otherwise

We must furnish each representative a list of these doubtful accounts so that she or he will know that their credit is shaky. *Otherwise,* our uncollectibles will continue to grow.

TO INDICATE TIME, PLACE, OR ORDER

above all, after all, again, finally, first, in the first place, further, in summary, meanwhile, next, still, then, too

It should not be surprising that Camden still has 60 percent of the market. *In the first place,* they have been in the hardware business twice as long as we have.

TO INTRODUCE EXAMPLES

for example, for instance, namely, that is, to illustrate

There are several ways in which the company can reduce travel expenses: *for example,* limiting representatives' calls to communities with a population of 3500 or over.

Sentence Fragments

We have all learned that to make sense, every sentence must have a subject and a predicate. Yet many people ignore this rule and produce no-sense sentences.

The exhibit materials are being sent to the hotel a week early. Which will eliminate the worry of their arriving late (as they did last year).

The second statement by itself makes no sense—it is a sentence fragment. We can fix the error in several ways. Here are two:

The exhibit materials are being sent to the hotel a week early, eliminating the worry of their arriving late (as they did last year).

The exhibit materials are being sent to the hotel a week early because I want to be sure they don't arrive late (as they did last year).

Following are other examples of sentence fragments.

WRONG

If the stock cards are posted daily, we will have up-to-date information that will be useful In many ways. Such as what items need to be reordered, what items are overstocked, and what items are moving slowly.

RIGHT

If the stock cards are posted daily, we will have up-to-date information that will be useful in many ways, such as what items need to be reordered . . .

WRONG

The duties of the service representatives vary considerably. Anything from writing up an order to arranging displays in the store.

RIGHT

The duties of the service representatives vary considerably, from writing up an order to arranging displays in the store.

Sometimes a sentence fragment is intentional—to add emphasis.

The sooner we can have a decision, the quicker we can solve the problem. This week?

The agency did admit that the proofreaders were somewhat careless in checking the copy for printer's errors. Obviously.

Philbin Associates Is one of the best accounting firms in Claremont. Perhaps *the* best.

Remember, however, that short, telegraphic sentences are effective only when they are used sparingly.

Your Turn

The following first paragraph of a memorandum contains sentence fragments. Rewrite, correcting these faults. (See page 191 for a suggested rewrite.)

Dear Mrs. Caulderwood:

The attached report on shrink-wrapping is being sent to all members of the Systems Group. Which is in response to your request of August 17. The report is in three sections. Consisting of requirements, methods, and cost.

Run-on Sentences

An even more common error in sentence construction is the run-on sentence—that is, a sentence with two complete thoughts that are not connected.

RUN-ON

Six designs were submitted, only two were approved.

CORRECT

Six designs were submitted, but only two were approved.

or

Six designs were submitted; only two were approved.

or

Of the six designs submitted, only two were approved.

RUN-ON

We had every intention of making the changeover in March, however, the equipment was not available.

CORRECT

We had every intention of making the changeover in March; however, the equipment was not available.

or

Although we had every intention of making the changeover in March, the equipment was not available.

Your Turn

Correct the following run-on sentences. (Revisions are on page 191.)

1. There were many staff problems in switching to cycle billing, nevertheless the system is now working very smoothly.
2. Staggering starting and quitting times caused some inconveniences at first, even so everyone seems content with the plan now.

Faulty Modifiers

Make sure to place modifiers close to the words they modify.

CONFUSING

We need the specialized services of an advertising agency thoroughly experienced in dealing with broadcast media to penetrate this market.

CLEAR

To penetrate this market, we need the specialized services of an advertising agency thoroughly experienced in dealing with broadcast media.

CONFUSING

The enclosed booklet· contains complete information about our products, prices, and discount policies that you may refer to when placing an order.

CLEAR

The enclosed booklet, which you may refer to when placing an order, contains complete information about our products, prices, and discount policies.

or

When placing an order, please use the enclosed booklet. It contains complete information about . . .

Even more serious is a dangling modifier—that is, an introductory phrase with nothing to modify. For example:

Driving down the Connecticut Turnpike, the Texaco sign was almost hidden by several large trees.

In the sentence illustrated, the writer took for granted that the reader would assume that a person was driving the car. Actually, though, it appears that the Texaco sign was driving.

Driving down the Connecticut Turnpike, *we noticed that* the Texaco sign was almost hidden by several large trees.

To avoid dangling modifiers, make sure that the action being described in the introductory phrase is performed by the subject of the sentence. If this isn't feasible, reword the sentence in some other way.

CONFUSING

In evaluating employees for salary increases in the upcoming payroll review cycle, employee productivity should be the main criterion. (It sounds as if "employee productivity" will do the evaluating.)

CLEAR

In evaluating employees for salary increases in the upcoming payroll review cycle, managers should use employee productivity as the main criterion.

CLEAR

Productivity should be the main criterion in evaluating employees for salary increases in the upcoming payroll review cycle.

Your Turn

Rewrite the following, solving the problems of faulty modifiers; then turn to pages 191-192 for suggested solutions.

1. The carton remained for three days on the loading dock, even though it was clearly marked "Perishable."
2. Each hostess wore a silk band on her wrist on which the word "Welcome" was printed in blue and yellow.
3. When flying on company business, first-class seats will be authorized only on transatlantic or transpacific flights.

Balanced Construction

Use parallel construction to present parallel ideas.

UNBALANCED

Telephone sales representatives should be pleasant, helpful, and exercise tact.

BALANCED

Telephone sales representatives should be pleasant, helpful, and tactful.

UNBALANCED

We believe it would be better to purchase a new printing press than trying to repair the present one.

BALANCED

We believe it would be better to purchase a new printing press than to try to repair the present one.

UNBALANCED

Ms. Farraday was hired as an instructor of shorthand and typewriting and to assist in preparing a secretarial manual.

BALANCED

Ms. Farraday was hired to conduct classes in shorthand and typewriting and to assist in preparing a secretarial manual.

YOUR TURN

Make the changes necessary for balanced construction and complete sentences; then turn to page 192 for a suggested solution.

Promoting and selling the company's product is a marketing function, while to develop a favorable company image is a public relations function. Although these functions often overlap between the two departments.

Omission of Words

Another error you see frequently in sentences is the omission of a word needed to preserve the sense of the sentence.

WRONG

Sales in July were as good, if not better than, in June.

RIGHT

Sales in July were as good *as,* if not better than, in June.

WRONG

The San Francisco plant is larger than any plant in this country. (Is it larger than itself?)

RIGHT

The San Francisco plant is larger than any *other* plant in this country.

WRONG

The supervisors have little experience and appreciation of the problems of leadership.

RIGHT

The supervisors have little experience *with* and appreciation of the problems of leadership.

Errors in Singulars and Plurals

Watch out for singulars and plurals; errors can distort meaning.

WRONG

I recommend that Bert Waldron and Phil Perkins be permitted to hire a secretary. (Assuming that each person will have a secretary.)

RIGHT

I recommend that Bert Waldron and Phil Perkins be permitted to hire secretaries.
or
I recommend that Bert Waldron and Phil Perkins each be permitted to hire his own secretary.

WRONG

Every supervisor in the factory should have their own office.

RIGHT

Every supervisor in the factory should have his or her own office.
or
All supervisors in the factory should have their own offices.

Correct the following sentence; then turn to page 192 for the solution.

I was pleased to have a report from both you and Ms. Bailey.
(Assume that there were two reports.)

Is the term *company* or *corporation* singular or plural? Technically, a company name is singular—one organization—even though it may contain a plural form. For example:

Lafayette Wholesalers *is* a relative newcomer to the home furnishings market, but it *is* coming on strong.

However, it is not uncommon to see the following:

Lafayette Wholesalers *are* relative newcomers to the home furnishings market, but *they* are coming on strong.

Although we prefer the first example, the second is acceptable. We do object, however, to "mixed" usages like this:

Lafayette Corporation *is* a relative newcomer to the home furnishings market, but *they* are coming on strong.

Sometimes an *of* phrase confuses writers in choosing a singular or plural verb. For example:

The main purpose of these reductions in travel expenses are not to cut costs but to encourage better planning of territory coverage.

No doubt you spotted the error quickly. The verb *are* should be *is,* since it relates to *purpose*—"The main purpose . . . is not to cut costs . . . "
Inverted sentences, where the subject *follows* the verb, also trip up some writers in dealing with verb number. Thus:

Among our advertising experts are a staff of three specialists in media evaluation.
Here the subject is *staff,* a singular noun that requires a singular verb:
Among our advertising experts *is* a staff of three . . .

Rewrite the following, correcting errors of word omission or in singulars and plurals. (See page 192 for suggested rewrite.)

1. Hodgkins is as successful—probably more so—than anyone in collecting overdue accounts
2. Opportunities for women are greater in the Waltham Corporation than in any corporation in our entire industry.
3. The focus of these studies have been on the reduction of turnover.

PARAGRAPHS

Many of the things we said about sentences apply to paragraphs as well.

Paragraph Length

Keep your paragraphs fairly short. Long paragraphs are discouraging to readers. To hold them, you must give them a "visual break" from time to time. You can usually do this by confining each paragraph to one big idea. Look at the following:

> Specialized industrial agencies, such as Dun & Bradstreet, are valuable sources of credit information. They provide detailed reports on thousands of firms, which include not only financial status and reliability but the company history as well. On the other hand, we should not overlook suppliers and vendors as sources of credit information. Indeed, information obtained from the credit departments of firms with which the applicant has had dealings is considered by many credit specialists to be the most reliable of all.

As you can see, the paragraph above has two major ideas: the use of industrial credit agencies and the use of credit departments of suppliers and vendors. So a new paragraph should be started after "company history as well."

Transition Between Paragraphs

Note that the transitional expression, *On the other hand,* begins the second paragraph. Obviously it is just as important to provide a bridge between paragraphs as between sentences.

YOUR TURN

The following is a memorandum on a new-employee induction program, the situation for which was described on page 27. As you read it, think of it as a rough draft that needs revising. Start the habit now of asking yourself, as you read your own communications and those you receive, What's wrong with this? How could it have been written better?

In the report that follows, you will find a lot of things wrong. There are sentence faults—fragments, run-ons, poor (or no) transitions. Some sentences and paragraphs are interminably long. Some are garbled. One word is misspelled/misused. The report needs more headings to break up copy. Jot down your ideas for revising the report or, better yet, redo it the way you think it should be. A suggested revision is on pages 192-194.

Worldwide Distributors Inc.

Interoffice Memorandum

To: Mrs. Cynthia Townsend

Dept: Personnel

Subject: A New-Employee Induction Program

From: Craig L. Bates

Dept: Personnel

Date: March 15, 19--

Dear Cynthia:

Here is the report you asked for on a new-employee induction program for Worldwide, which reviews the present procedure, describes the need for change, and presents a proposal for a new procedure.

PRESENT PROCEDURE

As you know, our present procedure for inducting new employees is brief and highly informal, one of us in Personnel giving employees a quick welcome, handing them a copy of "Worldwide's World," and escorting them to the departments where they will work--so there is really no program.

NEED FOR CHANGE

With the rapid growth of the company, it becomes more and more difficult for employees to learn about our various products, the markets we serve, the firm's objectives and future plans, and who we are and what we do, so there is no opportunity for new employees to meet top executives, learn about interdepartmental relationships, and find out how their own department fits into the total picture, plus the matter of educating employees about such things as compensation, retirement, fringe benefits, and general company policies, all of which are important not only in avoiding costly errors but also from the standpoint of general morale, meaning the sense of belonging and pride in being a part of the organization.

A NEW PROGRAM PROPOSAL

The weaknesses of the present procedure are obvious. Which calls for a more formal plan of induction, and I am suggesting that we establish a formal two-day induction program for all new employees. My plan calls for a twice-a-month program. Possibly the first and fifteenth. New employees are hired daily and therefore many would be placed on the job before going through the program. This is unavoidable, indeed this might be an advantage. Employees would have had an opportunity to get their bearings and thus be more receptive to formal induction. The major topics might be the following: Company history, which would be a brief account of the beginnings of Worldwide, its growth patterns, and its principle "shakers and movers"; a presentation of our products and services, with emphasis on markets served and our position in the market; the present structure of Worldwide, including the set-up of major divisions and how they interrelate; compensation, promotions and transfers, vacations, working hours, pay advances, sick leave, retirement plan, insurance, and various personal services; recreation, hobby groups, in-company and outside educational programs; special help to those who need special assistance on personal problems, legal and tax assistance, medical attention, etc.

Each program would be planned so that it is of maximum interest and inspiration, extensive use being made of audiovisual devices such as motion pictures, overhead projectors, tapes, flip charts, etc. Also, wherever possible, top executives would be asked to participate, selected "firing line" employees being asked to participate. Each participant would be carefully instructed on how to prepare the presentation, insisting that there be no long speeches and instead brief, interesting "show-and-tell" presentations. Finally, to the greatest extent possible, we would give

Mrs. Cynthia Townsend
Page 3
March 15, 19--

the new employees a chance to participate if they have been on
the job for a week or two.

THE FIRST STEP

I suggest that if you think this general proposal has merit you
ask to appear before the Executive Committee and the Operations
Committee meeting jointly to present the plan. Each division
executive might be asked to appoint a representative to serve
on a special Employee Induction Program Committee, the purpose
being to assist in the initial planning and then serving as a
standing committee to help manage the program.

FURTHER DISCUSSION

Please let me know if you wish to discuss this idea further.
Several articles and booklets have been obtained on induction
programs that you might like to see.

                                    Sincerely,

                                    C.L.B.

HIGHLIGHTS OF CHAPTER 3

1. Keep your sentences at a reasonable length.

   Checkup. Break down the following sentence into three of reasonable length. (See page 194 for a suggested rewrite.)

   An error in the inventory will lead to other erroneous figures in the balance sheet, such as total current assets, total assets, owner's equity, and the total of liabilities and owner's equity, as well as affect key figures in the income statement, such as the cost of merchandise sold, the gross profit on sales, and the net income for the period.

2. Avoid choppy sentences.

   Checkup. Rewrite the following, removing choppiness. (See page 194 for a suggested rewrite.)

   The title of the statistical table should be centered at the top. It should be as short as possible. Sometimes you need several words to identify the table. In this case, use a subtitle.

3. Use bridges (connectives) when necessary to tie your sentences together.

   Checkup. In the following there should be bridges between the sentences. See if you can supply them. (See page 194 for a suggested rewrite.)

   Almost any business can increase its sales if it does not consider the cost of selling. This is not realistic. In many companies, profit on sales is estimated before the sales are made.

4. Avoid sentence fragments except in special circumstances.

   Checkup. See if you can fix the following. (See page 194 for a suggested rewrite.)

   The carrier, according to the contract printed on the back of the bill of lading, is responsible for losses of or damages to merchandise. Which in the case of the Hooper shipment, amounts to about $3500.

5. Don't let your sentences run on.

   Checkup. Correct the following run-on sentence. (See page 194 for a suggested rewrite.)

   Fatigue and boredom both contribute to absenteeism, lack of incentive is also an important factor.

6. Place modifiers close to the words they modify.

   Checkup. Rewrite the following so that the meaning is clear. (See page 194 for a suggested rewrite.)

   The revenue is used in many different ways that is derived from sales taxes.

7. Beware of dangling modifiers.

   Checkup. Rewrite the following so that it is clear who is doing what. (See page 194 for a suggested rewrite.)

   Believing that production costs can be greatly reduced, computers now handle many operations that used to be done manually.

8. Use parallel constructions to present parallel ideas.

   Checkup. Rewrite the following sentence to achieve balanced construction. (See page 195 for a suggested rewrite.)

   Statistics can be used in hundreds of ways—for example, locating new markets, determination of population trends, the making of decisions concerning production quantities, comparisons between wages and prices, and deciding on new branch-store locations.

9. Watch for incorrect omission of words.

   Checkup. Insert the missing word in each of the following. (See page 195 for a suggested rewrite.)

   a. The production of energy-efficient heating systems is a project to which our engineers have and are giving much time and thought.
   b. Our Tarrytown plant produces more Widgets a year than any of our plants.

10. Make sure nouns and verbs agree.

    Checkup. Correct the following sentence. (See page 195 for a suggested rewrite.)

    In our warehouses are a wide variety of electronic equipment.

Writing believably

One of the most challenging report-writing assignments is that which requires you to investigate a problem or situation, make a thorough analysis of alternative solutions, then present your solution. Such reports are, more often than not, written at the request of someone higher up, and they pertain to such situations as these:

- Why have merchandise returns doubled in the fourth quarter?
- What would happen to sales revenue and profits if our trade discount rate to dealers was increased 5 percent?
- What would be the advantages, if any, of leasing automobiles for sales representatives rather than buying them?
- Why the high turnover in sales representatives this year?
- Is the huge amount of money spent on photocopying justifiable?

When making investigations and presenting alternative solutions, some writers get carried away, stating opinions as facts, using biased words and phrases, exaggerating, making quick generalizations from skimpy data, and puffing up a pet theory out of all reasonable proportions.

Let's look at an example. Arlington Industries' assistant sales manager has discussed with the marketing director the problem of maintaining an effective field force in the New England area. There has been considerable turnover in recent months, and most of those who resigned obtained positions with competitors. The regional managers in the three offices—Boston, Portland, and Burlington—have made their recommendations to the home office in Newark. The marketing director, however, wants the assistant sales manager to make a personal investigation and prepare a report of her findings and recommendations.

Suppose the report, which was based on interviews with regional managers, supervisors, and field representatives, contained the following statements.

1. The main reason we can't hold sales representatives is poor pay. Competitors are hiring away our people at a 20 percent higher salary than we pay.

2. The Boston office has a pathetically weak method of recruiting replacements. Believe it or not, the manager relies solely on other field representatives to obtain new representatives!

3. The turnover rate of field representatives in Portland is outrageously high, and the reason is definitely poor compensation.

And so on. The trouble with the statements illustrated, as you will see later, is that they are dogmatic. That is, the writer identifies opinions and hearsay as authoritative truths. Obviously, the writer did not intend to bend the truth, yet one might suspect it.

When you write reports in which you interpret information, make comparisons, arrive at conclusions, offer recommendations, and state opinions, your integrity is on the line. In these situations, you have to constantly ask yourself the question, Will my reader believe me? If your reader has reason *not* to believe you, your report is of little value. Besides, your personal image is tarnished.

BIAS IN REPORTS

In everyday life, all of us have pet biases about people, politics, clothes, colors, music, art, religion, and so forth. These biases are forgivable as long as they are not hurtful to others. It is not at all strange that biases are common in employment as well. The accountant, EDP specialist, sales representative, purchasing director, promotion manager, personnel executive are each expected to hold prejudices about his or her particular area of specialization and calibre of performance. Thus, the marketing person believes that everything in business revolves around sales; the accountant says that a business's success or failure boils down to intelligent financial planning and record keeping; the manufacturing manager believes a good showing in the market is the result of a great product rather than effective selling; and so on. Management is well aware of, and in general sympathy with, these biases, realizing that if people don't blow their own horn the organization has no spirit.

But biases can be carried too far. They are particularly dangerous in business reports. One obviously biased statement can destroy the reader's faith in everything else in the report. For example, one personnel supervisor, reporting the need for more people in the department, wrote: *The people in Personnel Relations work longer hours and are more dedicated to their jobs than those in any other department in the company.* Such a statement is almost impossible to prove; thus it is biased. It would have been a more honest and believable statement if the writer had said: *In my opinion, no group in the company works harder or is more dedicated than the Personnel Relations staff.*

As noted, some report-writing authorities maintain that a good report is always free of bias—that is, it must be "objective." This should generally be true of some reports, such as scientific studies and experiments, financial statements, engineering specifications, and straight statistical research papers. But there are opportunities, even in these situations, for interpretation and thus personal manipulation.

Executives often invite bias when they ask for reports. For example, suppose all the employees in a company are asked for their opinions of the firm's vacation policy. No one expects the respondents to be free of bias in this situation, and few people will view the matter impersonally.

But there are honest biases and there are deceptive biases. You are guilty of deceptive bias when you are expected to be objective and yet you attach prejudicial labels to people, systems, or procedures or slant your writing to embellish your viewpoint.

Attaching Labels

The dictionary is full of terms that can be used to bias a reader's opinion. Here are a few:

bureaucrats	military brass
big business	plush offices
inflated corporate profits	red tape
secret meetings	ivory tower
corporate conglomerates	vested interests
fat cats	big shots
power-hungry	eggheads
effete intellectuals	second-guessers
boondogglers	elitist
big wheels (management)	pressure groups

Equally destructive are terms that, standing alone, seem perfectly harmless, but can be sarcastic—even vicious—in certain contexts. For example:

ilk   Often used to identify a group whose opinions and/or conduct are not respected by the writer.

spurious   Usually refers to questionable data.

spiel   Describes a speech or conversation the author doesn't like.

secondhand   Sometimes used to identify information the writer objects to.

minutiae   Usually a snide reference to unnecessary detail.

ulterior   Used with "motive" to question another's intentions.

hot air   Same as for "spiel."

fad   A common way of describing a new system, procedure, or mode that the author doesn't like.

old-fashioned or outmoded   A label applied to almost anything the writer wants to see changed.

hush-hush   Refers to meetings or conversations from which someone (often the writer) was excluded.

The list of such expressions is long. People with whom we don't agree may be "hapless," "tactless," "insensitive," "callous," or having a certain "syndrome." Reference may be made to a difference of opinion as "Jones complained that," or "Jones alleged that," or "Jones claimed that." And those with whom we disagree may "bandy about" an issue rather than discuss it. Which leads us to the next topic: slanted writing.

Get rid of the biased expressions in the following sentences; then compare your revisions with those on page 195.

1. It is difficult to close the credibility gap between people in publicity, PR, promotion, and others of that ilk and those responsible for collections.

2. In her remarks about opportunities, Arlene gave a long spiel on the history of sex discrimination in this company.

3. It is clear that Zazzera used specious reasoning in his assessment of the brouhaha between the Accounting and Marketing departments.

4. The hubbub and furor over the new corporate logo is not only childish; it's inane.

5. Surely there is a more rational method than the one proposed by Personnel.

Slanted Writing

It is easy to slant our writing in such a way as to sway readers to accept a particular point of view. Let's look at the first paragraph of a newspaper report of a political rally:

> The turnout for Congressional hopeful Claud Zerbst last evening at Thalian Hall was pitifully sparse. Fewer than 400 hardy souls showed up to listen impassively to Zerbst's standard diatribe against "Washington politicians."

The reporter who wrote the above paragraph clearly is not a fan of the political figure Claud Zerbst. Did you spot the bias terms? *Congressional hopeful, pitifully sparse* (crowd), *fewer than 400 hardy souls, standard diatribe, "Washington politicians."*

Let's see how another writer, equally biased in the other direction, might have described the event:

> Claud Zerbst, dynamic young candidate for Congress, spoke last evening to an enthusiastic crowd of nearly 400 at Thalian Hall. Zerbst's insightful comments on the Washington political scene obviously excited the large audience, and his talk was interrupted time and again with roars of approval.

It is hard to believe, isn't it, that the two reporters attended the same rally? Every good reporter paints his or her own picture of a news event, giving color and interest to the story. One writer may refer to a public figure as "balding and middle-aged," while another calls him "seasoned." A tennis star who says little and plays with quiet determination is described by one reporter as "arrogant," by another as "imperturbable," and by a third as "enigmatic." We accept such labels in news writing as reflections of individual bias even though we may disagree with many of them.

In business report writing, however, you are expected to be more objective in stating your opinions. Some people think that objectivity is achieved when they eliminate personal pronouns—I, you, we, etc.—from their writing. This is not necessarily so. Compare:

WITHOUT PERSONAL PRONOUNS

Obviously a higher rate of productivity can be achieved by employing additional supervisory personnel.

WITH PERSONAL PRONOUNS

I think you will agree that we are likely to achieve greater production if we hire more supervisors.

One could argue that the statement at the right, though containing four personal references, is more objective than the one at the left, which has no personal pronouns but sounds dogmatic.

Nor do we achieve objectivity by pompous writing. For example:

WITHOUT PERSONAL PRONOUNS

It is believed that an incentive compensation plan for key personnel will result in greater efficiency, substantially improved economies, and high morale.

WITH PERSONAL PRONOUNS

I believe that an incentive compensation plan for key people will do three things for us: increase efficiency, save money, and improve morale.

The statement at the right is much easier to read than the one at the left, but it is no less objective.

We are not saying that all reports should reflect the writer's personality. Some writers think that reports based on research will be more believable if the style is somewhat formal. For example:

INFORMAL

I found it interesting that 35 percent of those who chose Brand Y over Brand X said they were influenced most of all by the package. Price wasn't even considered. So before we set up another testing situation, I think we ought to go with a new design—shape, texture, color, graphics, etc.

MORE FORMAL

Of the buyers who expressed a preference for Brand Y over Brand X, 35 percent indicated that packaging, not price, was the determining factor. It would appear, therefore, that before another test is conducted, an entirely new package might be . . .

Identifying Opinions as Opinions

Beware of stating opinions as facts. Unless you have undeniable proof of a claim or assertion, cover yourself with "hedge" statements such as the following:

* The results of this systems study *lead me to believe* that . . .
* *I think* more time should be given to sales training. *I base this opinion* on . . .

- Four of our seven promotion people (Day, Costello, Mannes, and Goralski) recommend that at least one/fourth of our budget should be spent on institutional ads. *I hold a different opinion, and my reasoning is this . . .*
- We have no proof that piped-in music increases factory production; personally, I find it offensive, and *I suspect* a number of others do too.
- Carpeting not only cuts down noise but, *according to the director of maintenance,* is easier to maintain than vinyl floor covering.

Your Turn

Tom Banker, a purchasing agent for an appliance manufacturer, has heard from three major suppliers (Wenco, Ramsey, and Consolidated) that there is likely to be a shortage of copper wire by the end of the year because of a prolonged strike in the industry. Banker wants to alert his boss to a potential problem and writes the following. Rewrite the statement, "hedging" rather than making factual declarations. (See the suggested solution on page 195.)

Because of the prolonged strike in the copper industry, we can expect to be caught short of copper wire if we do not place a large order now.

EXAGGERATION

The chief accountant rushes into the financial vice president's office saying, "Ellen, have you seen the sales figures for the first ten days? They're fabulous!" The vice president acknowledges the news accordingly. "Yes, Arthur, I agree—we're off to a terrific start."

Conversations such as this one are commonplace in business, even among top executives. Caught up in the enthusiasm that results from daily triumphs, most of us exaggerate when we speak, and such words as *fabulous* and *terrific* are accepted. In writing, however, such exaggerations are not acceptable. When ideas or data are recorded on paper, accuracy rather than overstatement is the rule. Thus, if the chief accountant were writing a report to the vice president about sales for the first ten days, he would be more likely to say something like this:

Sales for the first ten days of October were very good—40 percent over budget and 60 percent over last year.

In our "hard-sell" society, we see and hear terms in advertising that often stretch the truth: *fabulous selection, sensational styling, incredibly low priced, unbeatable deal, terrific values, unique* (or the illiterate "most unique") *features, once-in-a-life-time opportunity,* and *fantastic savings.* We accept them for what they are—sales puffs—and let them slide by without giving them much thought.

In business reports, however, exaggerations quickly destroy the writer's credibility. Be wary, then, of overstatements. Even when you can justify the use of such terms as *most, greatest, largest percentage, overwhelming majority,* and *fewest,* it is usually better to give specific data when you can. Here are examples.

1. *Most people in Blanford's like to have their salary checks mailed directly to their bank.* What does this mean? If there are 1000 employees and 519 of them want their salary checks mailed to their bank, is "most" an accurate word? Technically it is not inaccurate, but it is misleading. A safer statement would be, *Of the 1000 employees in Blanford's, slightly over 50 percent (519) want their checks mailed . . .*

2. *The overwhelming majority of our charge customers pay their accounts within 60 days of purchase.* What is an overwhelming majority—65 percent? 80 percent? 98 percent? If an exact percentage is known, it should be used. If not, the writer is much safer with something like this: *We estimate that between 70 and 80 percent of our customers pay their bills . . .*

3. *In our analysis, we found a significant difference in the number of units produced in September as compared with August.* What is a significant difference? Each reader will have her or his own idea what the term means—perhaps ranging from 10 percent to 100 percent—and it is better to be specific. *In our analysis, we found a significant difference in the number of units produced in September (over 1200) as compared with August (slightly under 900).*

4. *In the third quarter of this year alone, we lost six programmers; all received substantial increases in salary in their new jobs.* Again, what is a substantial increase? If the term "substantial" cannot be defined, it should be omitted. If it can be approximated, then a figure should be given. *In the third quarter of this year alone, we lost six programmers; all received substantial increases in salary—ranging from 15 percent to 25 percent—in their new jobs.*

5. *Bernard Croker is the best sales representative Murtaugh Distributors has ever had.* By what measurement? For many readers this statement will need to be qualified. *Ever since Murtaugh Distributors started business ten years ago, Bernard Croker has been number one in sales volume.*

6. *We received a large number of responses to our first advertisement in "National Viewpoint," leading us to believe that this might be a good medium for us.* How many is a large number? In relation to what? This is better: *Our first advertisement in "National Viewpoint" brought in 3500 responses—almost double that of any other similar medium. This leads us to believe that . . .*

7. *Several secretaries said that what they like least about their job is playing hostess—fetching coffee for visitors, for example.* How many is several? Is this the majority? About half? Only a few? This is more specific: *Of the twenty secretaries interviewed, seven said that what they like least about . . .*

8. *Only a few of the eighteen carburetors returned by Parker were actually defective.* More specific: *Of the eighteen carburetors returned by Parker, only four were actually defective.*

Fallacious Reasoning

Using fallacious reasoning and making rash generalizations will also erode believability in business reports. Here are examples.

1. *The Grand Forks region was 20 percent under its sales budget for the third month in a row. Therefore, we should add more representatives.* This reasoning is fallacious since there may be other reasons why sales are off—a slump in the economy, bad weather, heavier competition, poor selling, etc. If the writer believes the real reason is too few representatives, he or she should have said something like this: *The Grand Forks region was 20 percent under its sales budget for the third month in a row. This may be attributed to a number of things; however, we believe the main reason is that we don't have enough sales representatives to cover the territory adequately.*

2. *We spend too little on advertising. Our budget in Cavett Construction Company is less than half that of Martinson Electronics—and they don't even have our sales volume.* Such a statement is an example of "comparing apples and oranges." Missing in this type of reasoning is the possibility that an electronics firm must do more advertising than a building construction firm. The only valid comparison here would be with another construction business that deals in similar products, reaches the same markets, and is of comparable size.

3. *The great majority of gourmet restaurants have male chefs. Therefore, men are better cooks than women.* This is an example of a rash generalization based on inconclusive evidence. The fact that most chefs are men proves nothing. A more accurate statement would be: *Some of the best cooks in the world are men. Indeed, the great majority of gourmet restaurants have male chefs.*

4. *People are becoming increasingly resentful of receiving what they call "junk mail." Direct mail advertising, therefore, would not be a suitable medium for us.* Here the writer has drawn a specific conclusion from a broad generalization. Some people *are* resentful of junk mail, but the real test of direct mail advertising is not what people *say* they like or don't like, but how they actually respond to such advertising.

5. *Charles R. Maynard, in an article in the current issue of "Public Relations Review," says there is a definite trend among large companies toward turning the PR function over to outside agencies rather than attempting to handle the job themselves.*

Mr. Maynard's statement sounds convincing, but before it can be evaluated, we must know certain things about him:

1. Who is he? If he heads up a public relations firm that offers consulting services to various companies, his statement will be less impressive than if he were, say, a manufacturing corporation executive.

2. What is his authority? The term "definite trend" is often based on flimsy evidence.

3. Is his observation relevant? Mr. Maynard may have had reference to public utility corporations, which could have very little kinship with, say, automobile manufacturers or insurance companies.

Another way in which writers can slant their reports is by placing emphasis on the pros of their own argument and downplaying the cons. For example:

Although 60 percent of the employees questioned favored the new compensation arrangement, 35 percent were violently opposed to it.

It is possible that the 60 percent referred to were just as "violently" in favor of the proposed arrangement as the 35 percent who were opposed to it. Yet the writer obviously wants the reader to believe that it would be dangerous to install the new system.

Another writer who is in favor of the new compensation arrangement could just as easily color his or her argument thus:

> Fully 60 percent of the employees questioned favored the new compensation arrangement, while only 35 percent registered some opposition to it.

YOUR TURN

Rewrite the following sentence in such a way that it is more believable. (See page 195 for suggested rewrite.)

It is not surprising that our finance people always look at the bottom line first. Since they don't have the responsibility to produce those hard-earned sales, they apparently assume that money spent on design is sheer waste.

FALSE MODESTY

Although exaggerations and bias can be dangerous in business reports, excessive modesty is very nearly as bad. It is not wrong, of course, to exercise humility—especially when you're not an authority on the subject you are writing about—but don't overdo it. Excessive modesty will give your message a phony ring, even though it may be genuine. Here are examples.

1. *I am not an expert in education; therefore, my ideas about on-the-job training may not be valid. However . . .* Better: *My own experience in job training situations, reinforced by the comments many other trainees have made to me, leads me to make the following recommendations.*

2. *It may be presumptuous of me, a relative newcomer to Baroody's, to criticize the advertising policy of my predecessor, but . . .* Better: *I would like to see a new advertising policy established at Baroody's. Here are the reasons why I believe certain changes are in order.*

3. *I realize that I have little experience in supervision, but it seems to me that . . .* Better: *The people I've talked to—about thirty-five in six different departments—rate "fairness" as the principal quality of an effective supervisor. In second place is "job know-how."*

4. *Obviously a company as large as Consolidated doesn't need me to tell them how to improve public relations. However . . .* Better: *I have several ideas about improving Consolidated's public relations, and I would like to share them with you.*

5. *I appreciate the nice things you said about my slide presentation at the regional sales meeting. As you probably noticed, public speaking is not my forte . . .*
Better: *Thanks for the nice things you said about my slide presentation at the regional sales meeting. Your comments were a great boost to my self-confidence.*

YOUR TURN

Rewrite the following, eliminating the false modesty; then compare your version with that on page 195.

I'm not a forms expert and am therefore reluctant to make a suggestion on the proposed new job application form. However, I believe that even though the new form is a big improvement over the present one, you might possibly want to consider additional changes that may make the form even easier for applicants to fill out.

INSINUATIONS AND ACCUSATIONS

Another way to destroy rapport with your readers is to make insinuations and accusations, whether aimed at the recipient or at others. Examples follow.

1. *The credit manager claims that our sales representatives exercised poor judgment in interpreting credit policy to certain customers. This is an accusation with little substance. It is unfair to state exceptions as rules.* "Claim," "accusation," and "unfair" are harsh words and should be avoided. This is better: *The credit manager's statement that our sales representatives exercised poor judgment in interpreting credit policy to certain customers is not entirely accurate. This does happen, to be sure, but it is the exception rather than the rule.*

2. *It is hard to believe that the factory supervisors did not know about the new policy concerning overtime.* "It is hard to believe" suggests willful lack of conformance with policy. This is an improvement: *The new policy concerning overtime was the subject of several personnel memos, and we assumed that everyone was aware of it.*

3. *It is surprising that the receiving clerk did not notice the damaged articles at the time the carton was opened.* The phrase "It is surprising" accuses the receiving clerk of negligence or stupidity. Why not this: *Generally, damaged goods are quickly spotted by the receiving clerk when the carton is opened. Occasionally, however, there is a slip-up.*

4. *I fail to see the logic of items 4 and 7 in your recommendation.* There is a more tactful way to express a difference of opinion, such as: *I like the suggestions in items 1, 2, 3, 5, 6, and 8 in your recommendation. I do not agree, however, with 4 and 7, and here's why.*

5. *The purchasing director did not take the time, of course, to get competitive bids. If he had, he would have learned that . . .* This statement is loaded—"did not take the time" and "of course" are like hard punches to the midriff. This is better: *Competitive bids on this large installation would, it seems to me, have saved us a great deal of money.*

YOUR TURN

Rewrite the following sentences so that they are free of accusations and insinuations; then compare your revisions with those on pages 195-196.

1. In her report, Loftin overlooked the fact that commercial transportation cannot always be relied upon.
2. If Manufacturing had not delayed so long in providing final specifications, the packaging problem would have been solved by now.
3. Russell's excuse for exceeding the entertainment budget by 30 percent in April is absurd.
4. Maynard does have a legitimate alibi for the shipping delay; nevertheless, his failure cost us a big order.
5. The recruiting manager boasts of her record in filling personnel requisitions.

SARCASM

One of the surest ways to raise the dander of your reader is to show sarcasm when you are trying to make a point. Here are four examples:

1. *Congratulations! This is the third time this month the people in Shipping have mixed up a big order. Isn't this a new record?* Obviously the executive who wrote that is simply rubbing salt into already tender wounds. If he wants to issue a reprimand, this will do the job a lot better: *Mixing up the shipments this month of three of our most important customers is an obvious indication that some changes in procedures and/or personnel are badly needed. I want a complete report on the causes and the cures for these . . .*
2. *Sales figures for March show an industrywide growth of 15 percent. Our 10 percent decline makes the other fellows look pretty silly, doesn't it?* This derision hurts more than it helps. Let's try another approach: *I can understand our decline of 10 percent in sales for March. We've had these before, and generally they can be attributed to a soft market. But the industry as a whole showed a 15 percent INCREASE, so the market cannot be soft. I would be very much interested in your analysis of our poor showing.*
3. *Apparently the people in Personnel haven't yet discovered that we're in business to make a profit.* An insulting accusation, to be sure. This is more direct and adult: *Unfortunately, we simply can't afford all the new benefits you propose—not until our profit improves substantially.*

4. *Who else but the Office Services Division could have failed to get the word about the temporary moratorium on staff additions!* Why not the following instead? *The temporary moratorium on staff additions was announced in Executive Memo 17, dated June 14. According to our distribution list all managers and supervisors in your division got a copy of it.*

YOUR TURN

The writers of the following statements used sarcasm to put across their ideas. Rewrite them; then compare your statements with those on page 196.

1. Our sales performance in November can hardly be called stellar.
2. Computer errors plagued us again in September customer billings, but of course such errors are now the rule rather than the exception.
3. It's inconceivable that the purchasing manager chose not to follow our recommendations.
4. "Pathetic" is the only word that describes our retirement program.
5. Considering the appearance of our latest annual report, it is difficult to believe that we consider ourselves specialists in graphics!

TALKING DOWN TO READERS

Some writers can't resist the temptation to sermonize with their readers and issue banalities that insult their intelligence.

1. In our business it is important to attract and hold customers.
2. We must get the most from every dollar we spend for sales promotion.
3. The reputation of our business is paramount.
4. Good employee morale is important if we expect high productivity.
5. When we spend more than we receive, there is no profit.
6. Obviously, if we expect growth we must increase sales.
7. Surely by this time we have learned that customers expect and deserve fair treatment.
8. You should be able to understand that we cannot sacrifice quality for expediency.

ACCURACY IN WORD USAGE

Your credibility as a writer can be destroyed by using words incorrectly. Following are some common errors.

1. Hawkes and Muellner had typing speeds of 60 and 70 words a minute, *respect-fully*. (The correct word is *respectively*.)

2. They said they would complete the inventory *irregardless* of the heat. (The correct word is *regardless*.)

3. The employees felt that It was not an *equable* arrangement. (The right word is *equitable*; *equable* refers to something that is uniform or unchanging.)

4. The colors of the carpeting and drapes, though of different shades, are *com-plimentary*. (Use *complementary*.)

5. We certainly don't want a *reoccurrence* of the problem. (The correct word is *recurrence*.)

6. I will keep you *appraised* of the situation. (A common mistake; to appraise means to rate. The correct word is *apprised*.)

7. Did you mean to *infer* that Trakington was not the best applicant? (The correct word is *imply*.)

Hundreds of words are misused by business and government writers: *parameter* for *perimeter*, *imminent* for *eminent*, *accumulative* for *cumulative*, *disinterested* for *uninterested*, *forward* for *foreword*, *proscribe* for *prescribe*, *healthy* for *healthful*, and so on. Experienced writers keep a dictionary within easy reach and refer to it often. If you have not developed the dictionary habit, now is a good time to begin.

Equally dangerous are words and phrases used deliberately to conceal the truth. Government officials like to refer to a recession as a *static economic condition*, and corporation executives would rather talk about a *negative profit situation* than a loss. The word *situation* is often tacked on to phrases, presumably to soften the impact: *a surplus inventory situation*, *a soft market situation*, *a morale situation*, or *an over-budget situation*.

PRECISION IN WORD USAGE

Certain word usages, although not exactly inaccurate, are shunned by expert writers because they lack the preciseness desired. Here are three examples.

1. Most of the invoices will be mailed Thursday, and the *balance* on Friday. (A better word than *balance* is *rest* or *remainder*. Use *balance* to refer to a state of suspension ["hanging in the balance"] or to an amount ["Harrelson's account balance is $300."].)

2. The *bulk* of the orders went out yesterday. (In this case, *most* is preferable to *bulk*. Use *bulk* to refer to aggregates—bulk mailing, bulk rate, etc.)

3. If a better system is not devised, we are *liable* to lose money. (The word *liable* is not incorrect here, but because more often than not it refers to a legal obligation ["The court held Folsom liable for damages"], we prefer *likely* or *apt*.)

SEXISM IN REPORTS

Not long ago, in reports in which references were made to unnamed individuals, we saw only *he, his, him, man,* etc. For example:

> Training should be a continuous process. It should start when the *salesman* joins the company and continue as long as *he* remains a part of the sales force. Indoctrination training should be given as soon as *he* starts work; *he* must be given some basic training before *he* can be expected to do even a minimum job with customers. Refresher training should be given at intervals during *his* career. Continuous training by means of sales meetings and on-the-job training from *his* manager is a must for every *man.*

The writer of the passage above may have actually intended that the masculine references apply to both sexes. Today, however, it would be sharply criticized as sexist. And with considerable justification; after all, there are many successful women sales representatives in business. Now, we are more likely to say this:

> Training should be a continuous process. It should start when the sales *representative* joins the company and continue as long as *he or she* remains a part of the sales force. Indoctrination training should be given as soon as the *representatives* start work; *they* must be given some basic training before *they* can be expected to do even a minimum job with customers. Refresher training should be given at intervals during *their* career. Continuous training by means of sales meetings and on-the-job training from managers should be a regular affair.

You will see that it can be awkward to include both sexes in every reference. Using *he or she, she/he,* etc., over and over becomes labored and somewhat silly. The answer is to reword your presentation, using the plurals *they* and *them* and omitting a reference to gender when it is not really needed. Note the omission of such references in the rewriting of the closing of the first example. Compare:

> . . . by means of sales meetings and on-the-job training from *his* manager is a must for every *man.*
> . . . by means of sales meetings and on-the-job training from managers should be a regular affair.

Obviously, when reference is made to a specific individual, sex identification is required:

1. Frank Olsen said he would do everything he could to improve the schedule he proposed in July.
2. In her report on company donations, Eileen Murfree recommended that she or another representative from Public Relations head up the screening committee.

YOUR TURN

See if you can eliminate the sexist statements in the following paragraph; then compare your version with that on page 196.

At the conclusion of his audit, the internal auditor will submit his written report identifying the objective and scope of his study, the methods he used, and his findings. His report should not only show the number, percent, and type of errors, but also include his recommendations for improvement. Remember, the auditor's job is to advise a supervisor of his shortcomings. It is the supervisor's responsibility to follow through once his shortcomings are pointed out.

REPORT OF AN INVESTIGATION

At the beginning of this chapter, we described a situation in which the assistant sales manager of Arlington Industries was asked to look into a personnel problem in the New England area. This person was to pay a visit to the three regional offices, get at the heart of the problem, and recommend ways of solving it.

The following report violates many of the principles of good reporting that were discussed in this chapter and earlier. Read it carefully, asking yourself as you read: What's wrong with this report? How can it be made better? Look especially for the following:

1. Sentence faults
2. Businessese and federalese expressions
3. Opinions stated as facts
4. Bias words
5. Awkward writing
6. Improper word usage (there is only one instance of this)
7. Insinuations, accusations, and sarcasm
8. Slanted writing
9. Exaggerations
10. Fallacious reasoning

Since you did not make the trip to New England and do not know all the circumstances, finding all the "horrors" in the report won't be easy. But even if you spot a half dozen or so, your time will have been well spent. When you have made your analysis, take a careful look at the more acceptable report on pages 63-67.

Arlington Industries

Interoffice Memorandum

To: D. J. McIntyre

From: K. C. Spengler

Subject: Visit to New England Regional Offices

Date: October 14, 19--

Pursuant to your request, a week was spent in each of the New England regional offices--Boston, Burlington, and Portland-- where interviews were conducted with the three regional managers and seven field supervisors concerning the problem of maintaining a productive field force therein. Interviews were likewise carried on between myself and 15 field representatives. Following is a brief report.

BOSTON

Boston, when at full complement, has 28 field representatives and four field supervisors. Generally speaking, it is a strong group, since June, however, four representatives have resigned to accept positions with Globe Products at considerably higher salaries:

> Charles Persons (Hartford)
> Nancy Comiskey (Providence)
> David Silberstrom (New Bedford)
> Samuel Hotchkiss (Springfield)

A fifth representative, Elizabeth Conway (Bangor), will undoubtedly leave momentarily.

Reasons for Resigning

The reasons why these people are resigning are similar:

1. Financial--low basic salary, poor incentive plan, and low mileage allowance

2. Supervision--field supervisors are too demanding and communicate poorly with the representatives

3. Opportunities--failure of the company to recognize quality
   performance and provide equitable opportunities for advancement

Replacement Efforts

Although the Boston office has tried to recruit new representatives to replace resignees, no progress is evident. Surprisingly,
the method of recruiting people is confined to word-of-mouth
recommendations of other field representatives.

The Remaining Staff

There is obviously a growing unrest among the remaining representatives, and they were especially vociferous about poor
compensation. No fewer than five representatives gave this as
the principal consideration in their unhappiness. Four acknowl-
edged a problem of getting along with their field supervisor.
Two complained bitterly about the lack of advancement opportunities and recognition by management.

BURLINGTON

Although Burlington is fully complemented at the moment (12
representatives and 2 field supervisors), it's a foregone conclusion that we will lose Capaletti in Burlington and Mintz in
Keene, both are excellent performers. The problem is money,
both have been offered jobs with other firms (Stedman Inc. and
Pryor Manufacturing, respectfully) at a higher salary--Capaletti,
20 percent higher. Neither mentioned any other consideration,
indeed they like their work, their field supervisors, and the
company.

D. J. McIntyre
Page 3
October 14, 19--

The Remaining Staff

The rest of the Burlington field force is intact and productive, and the fantastic growth of this region confirms the general contentment of the field representatives. Morale is excellent. I was frequently asked the question, What can you do about getting more money for me?

Recruiting

Burlington won't have any difficulty recruiting new representatives, the regional manager having established exceptionally good relations with institutions of higher education in the area and obtains impressive candidates from these sources.

PORTLAND

The Portland office is at full complement except one vacancy, however, the regional manager has had several promising interviews, so the vacancy will be filled before the end of this month. However, the situation here is perilous. Mainly because of turnover.

Turnover

Portland has had good luck filling its vacancies, but the turnover rate is shocking. Of the 15 representatives in this region, seven have been with the company less than a year (!), four less than two years, and only one more than five years. Compensation is the big reason for turnover. (This is confirmed by the regional manager's notes at the exit interviews.) Secondarily, lack of opportunities for advancement; and a tertiary reason is dictatorial field supervision and lack of recognition.

D. J. McIntyre
Page 4
October 14, 19--

"Communication Gap"

There is definitely a communication gap between home office personnel and field personnel. The field supervisors and representatives are convinced that they are being totally ignored
by the home office in Newark.

SUMMARY

We are faced with three basic problems in the New England area.
Importancewise, they are:

1. Compensation--basic salary, incentives, increases, and
    expense allowances

2. Recognition--acknowledgment of good work, promotional oppor-
    tunities, and evidence of awareness

3. Supervision--bad supervision, bossy supervisors, and
    ridiculous demands

Obviously, these three problems overlap one another. Certainly
it is all too frequent that when people gripe they can be sus-
pected of not telling the truth. It is apparent to me that if
these complainers were given recognition by the big shots in
Newark, there wouldn't be any problem.

RECOMMENDATIONS

The situation in New England is desperate and calls for immediate and drastic action:

1. Salary Study. The company should make an immediate study
of salaries and incentives, including a comparison with figures
in the industry and in similar firms within each demographic
entity. It is mandatory that the incumbent representatives are
made aware that such a study is a highly prioritized matter.

D. J. McIntyre
Page 5
October 14, 19--

2. Supervisory Training. A supervisory improvement program should be instituted at once for all field supervisory personnel. Which would be conducted in the regional offices, utilizing from outside the company a qualified instructor. (Professor Wolff from the Harvard Business School would be ideal.)

3. Management Contacts. Critically important is more frequent contacts between management and field personnel. Three ways in which these contacts should be effectuated are:

    a. The marketing director, along with other top executives in the company, should attend every regional sales conference.

    b. Key executives must acknowledge outstanding performance by field personnel, writing congratulatory letters.

    c. A monthly field representatives newsletter should be published, for it would certainly close the communication gap.

4. Recruitment Conference. Conduct a conference in each regional office for the purpose of instructing managers and other personnel on the techniques of recruiting, interviewing, and employing representatives. This should be done under the aegis of our Personnel Department.

R.C.S.

Arlington Industries

Interoffice Memorandum

TO: D. J. McIntyre   FROM: K. C. Spengler

SUBJECT: Visit to New England Regional   DATE: October 14, 19--
Offices

At your suggestion, I spent a week in each of the New England regional offices--Boston, Burlington, and Portland--where I talked with the three regional managers and seven field supervisors about the problem of maintaining a productive field force. I also interviewed 15 field representatives. Following is a brief report.

BOSTON

When at full strength, Boston has 28 field representatives and four field supervisors. Generally speaking, it is a strong group. However, since June four representatives have resigned to accept jobs with Globe Products, reportedly at considerably higher salaries:

Charles Persons (Hartford)   Nancy Comiskey (Providence)
David Silberstrom (New Bedford)   Samuel Hotchkiss (Springfield)

A fifth representative, Elizabeth Conway (Bangor), has indicated her intention of leaving.

Reasons Given for Resigning

The three main reasons these four people gave for resigning are:

1. Financial--low basic salary, poor incentive plan, and low mileage allowance

2. Supervision--lack of rapport with the field supervisor

3. Opportunities--failure of the company to recognize their worth and provide opportunities for advancement

Here we eliminated two businessese terms—*pursuant to* and *therein*. By using the personal pronoun *I,* we eliminated the stuffiness, making the copy more readable and more interesting.

In the original report, the second sentence in this paragraph was a run-on. Here there are two sentences.

Because we're not positive that the four representatives have been promised higher salaries by Globe Products, we think it wise to insert the disclaimer word *reportedly*.

Notice that we have softened the writer's dogmatic statement about Elizabeth Conway to *has indicated her intention of leaving*. Since there is no evidence that Conway has actually resigned, there may still be a chance that she will stay.

Minor editing was done here, mainly to clarify meaning and to remove deadwood. The statement about supervision was rewritten; it seemed harsh. *Lack of rapport with the field supervisor* is fairer to the field supervisors.

D. J. McIntyre
Page 2
October 14, 19--

Replacement Efforts

Although the Boston office has tried to recruit new representatives to replace those who resigned, there is little progress
to report. Incidentally, the method of recruiting people seems
to be confined to word-of-mouth recommendations of other field
representatives.

The Remaining Staff

The four field supervisors, as well as the regional manager,
feel that there is a growing unrest among the remaining representatives. They cite compensation as the principal reason.
The five representatives I talked with confirmed this. However, four also mentioned the problem of getting along with
their field supervisor. Two cited lack of advancement opportunities and recognition by management as major concerns.

BURLINGTON

Burlington is fully staffed at the moment (12 representatives
and 2 field supervisors). However, it seems almost certain
that we will lose Capaletti in Burlington and Mintz in Keene-
both excellent performers. Again the problem appears to be
money; both say they have been offered jobs with other firms
(Stedman Inc. and Pryor Manufacturing, respectively) at a
higher salary--Capaletti indicated 20 percent higher. Neither
mentioned any other consideration. Indeed, they like their
work, their field supervisors, and the company.

The Remaining Staff

As far as I can determine, the rest of the Burlington field
force is intact and productive, and the growth of this region
would seem to confirm the general contentment of the field

Here we replaced the strange word *resignees* with *those who resigned.* We also think *there is little progress to report* is more tactful than *no progress is evident.*

In the original report, the word *Surprisingly,* which begins the second sentence, seems sarcastic. We've substituted *Incidentally.*

It seemed to us that in the original memorandum the author overreacted to the situation, so the language was softened. *No fewer than five* shows evidence of slanted writing, and that phrase was eliminated.

In the original report, the writer's phrase *foregone conclusion* leaves no room for doubt. We prefer the "hedge" phrase *it seems almost certain.* This sentence also corrects the run-on in the original version.

Note the hedges. Instead of *The problem is money,* we say *The problem appears to be money;* instead of *Capaletti, 20 percent higher,* we think it's better as *Capaletti indicated 20 percent higher* since we have only his or her word for it. The last sentence was a run-on and is now two sentences.

If you compare the original of this paragraph with the revision, you will see that we have chosen less definitive language. Has the region's growth been "fantastic"? Does this growth confirm the general contentment of the field representatives or merely seem to?

Revision   **Comments**

D. J. McIntyre
Page 3
October 14, 19--

representatives. Morale seems generally good, although I was
frequently asked the question, What can you do about getting
more money for me?

Is morale "excellent" or does
it seem generally good?

A bridge is needed between
the last two sentences, such
as *however* or *although*.

Recruiting

Burlington is not likely to have difficulty recruiting new
representatives. The regional manager has established exceptionally good relations with colleges and universities in the
area and obtains good people from these institutions.

We can't be positive that
Burlington won't have any
difficulty in recruiting, so
we've softened the
statement. We also broke this
paragraph down into two
sentences and simplified the
language, which seemed
high-flown.

PORTLAND

The Portland office is short one representative, but the regional
manager has had several promising interviews and believes the
vacancy will be filled before the end of this month. The situation here, however, is not as rosy as might be imagined.

In the original, the first
sentence was a run-on and
the last a fragment. These
corrections, plus
straightening out awkward
construction, makes the
revised paragraph easier to
read. Dogmatic statements
were also revised.

Turnover

While Portland seems to have little trouble filling its vacancies, the turnover rate is extremely high. Of the 15 representatives in this region, seven have been with the company less
than a year, four less than two years, and only one more than
five years. According to notes made by the regional manager
at the exit interviews, compensation is the main reason for
turnover. Next in importance is lack of opportunities for
advancement, followed by "dictatorial field supervisor" and lack
of recognition.

The word *shocking* in the
original appears to be an
exaggeration and the (!)
following *less than a year*
sarcastic. In general, we have
toned down strong assertions
in this paragraph, including
putting quotation marks
around the phrase *dictatorial
field supervisor.*

"Communication Gap"

The field supervisors, as well as the representatives, made frequent reference to the "communication gap" between home office
people and field people. "Does anybody in Newark know we're
out here?" is a recurring question.

There seems to be no good
reason for the big words
secondarily and *tertiary* in the
original, and this material was
rewritten. Indeed, the last
sentence was garbled and
now is easier to read.

Again, in the original of this
paragraph the writer seems to
have overreacted, and we
softened the language.
Although there's nothing
really wrong with the word
personnel, we prefer to use
people when it will do just as
well.

D. J. McIntyre
Page 4
October 14, 19--

SUMMARY

From this rather informal study, I would say that we are faced
with three basic problems in the New England area. In order
of importance, they are:

1. Compensation--basic salary, incentives, increases, and
    expense allowances

2. Recognition--acknowledgment of good work, promotions, and
    "attention" in general

3. Supervision--lack of rapport with field supervisors,
    "overmanagement," and excessive demands

Obviously, these three problems overlap one another. Also,
what people give as reasons for discontent may not be actually
in the order listed. I have the impression, although I have
no documentation, that if the "nobody cares" complaint were
resolved, the two other problems would diminish in importance.

RECOMMENDATIONS

Although the situation in New England is far from hopeless, it
seems to me to be serious enough to suggest that we take some
positive steps immediately. I recommend the following:

1. Salary Study. A study of salaries and incentives, including a comparison with figures in the industry and in similar
firms within each geographical area, should be undertaken. All
representatives in the New England area should be made aware
that such a study is under way.

2. Supervisory Training. A "how to supervise" training program for all supervisors would, it seems to me, be very useful.
This program might be held in the regional offices, using a
qualified instructor from outside the company. (A possibility
is Professor Wolff from the Harvard Business School.)

The qualification, *From this informal study, I would say,* is wise, for it characterizes the writer as cautious instead of rash.

Importancewise* is a foolish word, definitely in the federalese category. Why not *In order of importance?

In the original, the items following *Recognition* seemed vague. Also, the negative words following *Supervision* appeared to be unnecessary. We think these statements are clearer and more reasonable.

There was no excuse in the original for the writer to get into the ugly accusation that perhaps the representatives lied or to use such words as *gripe, complainers,* and *big shots.* Here the author lost yardage when points could have been scored. Notice how much more reasonable—and clearer—the revision is.

The term *ideal* to describe Professor Wolff seems gratuitous. We prefer *possibility.*

Based on what we read in the original report, we see little evidence that the situation in New England is "desperate," as the author claims, calling for "drastic" action. The revised statement seems more rational.

Besides waving a red flag, the author used some businessese terms that we eliminated— *demographic entity, incumbent,* and *prioritized.*

In our revision, we have been less demanding than the author in the original version. Note our substitutions for the terms *supervisory improvement program, field supervisory personnel, conducted,* and *utilizing.*

D. J. McIntyre
Page 5
October 14, 19--

3. Management Contacts. More frequent contacts between management and field people seem critically important. Here are three
ways that may be used to close the so-called "communication gap".

    a.   The marketing director, along with other top executives
        in the company, should try to attend as many regional
        sales conferences as possible.

    b.   Key executives might be encouraged to acknowledge out-
        standing performance by field personnel with congrat-
        ulatory letters.

    c.   A monthly newsletter, written expressly for field
        representatives, could be an effective communication
        medium.

4. Recruitment Conference. It might be productive if a conference were held in each regional office, under the supervision
of our Personnel Department, to instruct managers and others
on the techniques of recruiting, interviewing, and hiring
representatives.

K.C.S.

The revision of the remaining
copy of the original report
concentrates on suggesting
rather than demanding. Who
is to say that the marketing
director and other top
executives *should attend
every regional conference?*
Or that key executives *must*
write congratulatory letters?
Nor can we be certain that a
monthly newsletter for field
representatives will close the
communication gap.

Note in the final paragraph
that we have substituted the
word *supervision* for the
author's *aegis.*

HIGHLIGHTS OF CHAPTER 4

1. Don't let bias destroy your credibility.

   Checkup. Rewrite the following, removing obvious bias. (See the suggested rewrite on page 196.)

   a. Our advertising campaign was so effective that there was virtually no need for personal selling.

   b. Systems analysts have a habit of deciding on the input to be recorded without reference to management needs.

2. Don't attach labels to people or procedures to shoot them down.

   Checkup. Identify the labels in the following sentences; then rewrite the copy so that it is more objective. (See the suggested rewrite on page 196.)

   a. I suggest that we give all these girl Fridays a solid course in English grammar.

   b. Your informants twisted the facts about the high cost of the new corporate logo.

3. Avoid slanted writing.

   Checkup. Rewrite the following to remove evidence of obviously slanted writing. (See the suggested rewrite on page 196.)

   I hope we don't succumb to the disease of "acquisition mania," which has afflicted so many corporate types.

4. Don't state opinions as facts.

   Checkup. The following statements are dogmatic. Soften them. (See the suggested rewrite on page 196.)

   a. I am convinced that the only feasible location for a new distribution center in the Chicago area is Northbrook.

   b. It is clear that these four distributors intentionally violated our dealer discount policy.

5. Beware of overstatements.

   Checkup. Rewrite the following so that it is more believable. (See the suggested rewrite on page 196.)

   We have had incredible success this year in the Canadian market. Sales in the third quarter enjoyed a whopping boost over the same period last year—a fantastic achievement

6. Don't use fallacious reasoning and rash generalizations.

   Checkup. The following sentence contains a generalization that is hard to prove. Fix it. (See the suggested rewrite on page 196.)

   Factory absenteeism on Monday, the 24th, was extremely high, attributable no doubt to "Super Sunday."

7. Avoid false modesty.

   Checkup. Rewrite the following so that it doesn't sound like groveling. (See the suggested rewrite on page 196.)

   Although the Inspection Department made more than its share of mistakes last year, our modest improvement in the first quarter of this year will surprise you, as it did me.

8. Be wary of insinuations and accusations.

   Checkup. Rid the following sentence of insinuations. (See the suggested rewrite on page 196.)

   The Purchasing Section's infatuation with certain long-time suppliers makes one wonder whether we're really getting the best quality at a fair price.

9. Shun sarcasm.

   Checkup. In the following sentence, the writer uses sarcasm to prove a point. Rewrite it. (See the suggested rewrite on page 197.)

   Of course, knowing Peterson, we can be certain that his motive is "completely altruistic."

10. Don't talk down to your readers.

    Checkup. In the sentence that follows, a personnel manager talks down to employees in the department. Revise it. (See the suggested rewrite on page 197.)

    Let's not forget that the word personnel is just another name for people. We must not lose sight of the fact that the business of the Personnel Department is people.

11. Use words correctly.

    Checkup. Two words are used incorrectly in the following sentence. Substitute the correct ones. (See the suggested rewrite on page 197.)

    From Clausen's comment, I deduct that she thinks we have not been discrete in handling confidential credit information.

12. Avoid sexism in your writing.

    Checkup. The following paragraph is sexist. Rewrite it for better balance. (See the suggested rewrite on page 197.)

    Before a work measurement program is begun, the supervisor should be thoroughly briefed. He must have a good understanding of it if he is expected to cooperate. He must also be in a position to explain and help to sell the program to the clerical people reporting to him. The supervisor's secretary is a key person too. She must know as much as her boss and help him put the idea across to others.

Selling your ideas

Many, if not most, of the reports you write will be for the purpose of selling an idea or a point of view to a superior or a committee. These reports are usually written on interoffice stationery.

Preplanning is important for every report you write, but it is critical in "selling" reports. Effective sales technique requires you to prepare your case just as carefully as a lawyer who is getting ready to defend a client. He or she bones up on every facet of the case, leaving little room for last-minute surprises. This means, for one thing, anticipating what the other side is going to say and do, bringing to mind the old rule of sports, "The best defense is a good offense."

So when you are considering selling an idea to someone higher up, think through the situation carefully, anticipating every possible objection. (There are always objections, particularly when your idea means spending money!) And, most important, prepare an outline before you start to write. A good sales representative, in getting ready to land that big order, goes through several mental rehearsals before facing the customer. The report-writer's rehearsal takes the form of a carefully constructed outline, which may be revised again and again as she or he tries to read the mind of the person to whom the idea is being presented.

Let's look at two examples.

EXAMPLE 1: SELLING THE NEED FOR AN INCREASE IN STAFF

The manager of the Customer Services Unit of Kinghoff Company is greatly concerned about the backlog of unanswered letters from customers and prospective customers. The volume of mail has increased substantially over the past year, and the present staff of three correspondents is unable to keep up with it. The manager of the unit, J. R. Barringer, decides to ask for authorization to hire an additional correspondent. There is one big obstacle: because profits this year are well below expectations, all executives have been directed by the president to hold the line in hiring additional personnel.

Barringer, although well aware of the challenge he faces, is so desperate that he fires off the following memorandum to the vice president, C. T. Jessup.

MEMORANDUM
Kinghoff Company ═══════

TO: Mr. C. T. Jessup   FROM: J. R. Barringer

SUBJECT: Customer Services   DATE: August 3, 19--

This unit needs an additional sales correspondent desperately.
Not only are we ten days behind with our correspondence to
customers and prospective customers, we're getting further and
further behind every day. Although I have tried everything I
know to alleviate the situation, I am convinced that there is
no hope of solving this problem with our present staff.

In view of these circumstances, I trust I have your permission
to add another correspondent.

J.R.B.

If by now you have developed the habit of looking critically at everything you write or receive, you will quickly spot what's wrong with the memorandum shown. Although Barringer's writing is fine, including tone and style, he has not achieved his objective, which is to persuade Jessup to say yes to the request for a staff addition.

The following questions will help you spot the weaknesses in the memo:

1. Is the subject properly identified?
2. Has Barringer supplied all the facts Jessup will need to make an intelligent decision?
3. Has Barringer anticipated objections from Jessup?
4. Is cost properly dealt with?
5. Besides cost, what else is Jessup likely to ask about?
6. Has Barringer given Jessup any help in case Jessup has to try to sell the idea to the president?
7. If you were Jessup, how would you react to the last paragraph?

If Barringer had bothered to think through thoroughly the problem both he and Jessup face, he would have produced an altogether different report. He would have prepared a working outline before he started to write, which might have looked something like this:

    A. Need for additional correspondent

        1. Present staff production

        2. Growth of correspondence (suggest why)

B. Attempts to solve problem

(List methods used to routinize—printed forms, form letters and paragraphs, automatic typewriters, letter shops, overtime)

C. Customer complaints (indicate the consequences of delayed responses)

D. Cost

1. New correspondent's salary (net)
2. Potential loss of business

E. Recommendation

(Hire Judith Ustinov)

SUGGESTED REVISION

Now let's look at the report Barringer might have written if he had done his homework. Pay particular attention to the comments at the right.

Revision

Comments

MEMORANDUM
Kinghoff Company

TO: Mr. C. T. Jessup   FROM: J. R. Barringer

SUBJECT: Need for Additional Sales   DATE: August 3, 19--
Correspondent

I would like your authorization to add another sales correspondent to the Customer Services Unit staff. My request is based on considerations that are likely to affect sales performance directly in the months ahead.

NEED

As you know, we now have three experienced sales correspondents, each of whom can handle about 25 letters a day, assuming the letters concern fairly routine matters. In a typical month of 22 working days, then, we can process about 1650 pieces of correspondence.

During the past twelve months the volume of customer correspondence has increased upwards of 50 percent. Now instead of receiving from 1500 to 1800 customer inquiries a month, we are averaging between 2400 and 2700. The difference can be accounted for, no doubt, by the greater sales volume and the number of new product lines that are being added. But whatever the reason, we have more correspondence than we can handle with our present staff.

The subject of the memorandum is now accurately stated.

The suggestion of a negative effect on sales performance adds strength to the opening request.

In a selling report, failure to supply specific data is almost certain to result in "no sale." Jessup will need this information if he has to sell the idea upstairs.

ATTEMPTS TO SOLVE THE PROBLEM

We have tried several ways to handle the correspondence volume
with our present staff:

1. We have reduced the amount of outgoing correspondence to
    the absolute minimum. When a written communication is not
    actually called for, we don't send one.

Jessup will undoubtedly want to know what Barringer has done to solve the problem without increasing his staff. On this point, specificity is a must.

Mr. C. T. Jessup
Page 2
August 3, 19--

2. For the most routine situations, we have had acknowledg-
    ments and similar messages printed.

3. Where personal responses are required, we often use form
    letters and form paragraphs, eliminating dictating time.

4. When several personalized communications that contain the
    same message are required, we make use of automatic type-
    writers and other word processing equipment.

5. Some of the correspondence has been farmed out to local
    letter shops, but this has proved very costly and unsatis-
    factory.

6. Several company employees have been engaged on an overtime
    basis.

CUSTOMER COMPLAINTS

In the past two weeks I have had 18 memos and telephone calls
from sales representatives who have had complaints from customers
and others about our slowness in answering letters. Seven
customers wrote or called directly; five threatened to cancel
their orders. So the situation is serious.

This brief statement anticipates the question, So what if we're a few days behind answering letters?

COST

We are now paying between $15,000 and $20,000 a year to our
present correspondents. I believe we can obtain a new correspondent for a salary of $14,000 a year; fringe benefits and space
costs will amount to about $6,200 a year. The actual net cost,
however, would be considerably less than $20,200 a year since
we could eliminate overtime and service charges of outside
agencies, which now average $900 a month.

In determining the cost, we must also consider the potential
loss of business because of unhappy customers. I have no way

Nothing is more important in a selling report than answering the question, How much? It is on this critical issue that many executives base their decision.

Mr. C. T. Jessup
Page 3
August 3, 19--

of estimating this, but I have the feeling that, in time, the
amount could be very substantial.

**Opinions are carefully labeled
as such.**

RECOMMENDATION

If you agree with me that it is essential that we add a correspondent to our staff, I recommend that we promote Judith
Ustinov to that position. Judith is executive assistant to
Lloyd Fuchs, sales manager, and has performed most capably for
the past three years. She is well acquainted with our products
and our service policies and has demonstrated a fine writing
ability. I believe that with a minimum amount of training
Judith could quickly assume her share of the correspondence
load.

**A specific recommendation is
expected, but it is low key.**

I have discussed this matter on a confidential basis with Lloyd,
and he would be willing to release Judith because of the promotion this job represents. Although she has indicated informally her interest in becoming a sales correspondent, I have
not, of course, discussed this position with her.

**Note that Barringer is careful
to say that he has made no
overtures to Judith Ustinov.
Such a move would wipe out
any hope of selling the idea to
Jessup.**

YOUR TURN

Let's say that you manage a department in your company where there
is a good deal of correspondence with stockholders. Unfortunately, the
six typewriters in the department are fairly ancient electrics, and you
want to replace them with new electronic machines. What do you think
of the following as an outline of a report to your boss requesting this new
equipment? (Your boss hates to spend money.)

1. Appearance of department not good because of condition of present
   typewriters

2. Almost all other departments in the company have newer, better typewriters

3. Features of the new electronics (supply color brochures left by typewriter
   representatives)

4. Can get delivery in two weeks

If the outline above doesn't satisfy you, jot down your own and compare it with the one on page 197.

EXAMPLE 2: SELLING THE NEED FOR A NEW DEPARTMENT

Let's look at another example of a selling report. Here is the situation. The controller of Northwest Leather Goods, a fast-growing enterprise, believes the company is wasting time and money with its present purchasing system. The twelve divisions in the company do their own buying of supplies and equipment for internal use, and the controller, Carolyn Amend, wants to see the purchasing function centralized. On her own initiative, she analyzes the problem and decides to write a report to the president.

The controller feels strongly about the need for a centralized purchasing system and wants to sell it. As mentioned, when you want to sell an idea to somebody upstairs, you approach the matter much as good sales representatives tackle an important buyer who has doggedly avoided consideration of their product in the past. They make it a point to know everything there is to know about their own product as well as the competitor's. (In this case, your product is your idea; the "competitor's" product consists of all the obstacles you face, particularly cost.) Both you and the sales representative plan your presentation carefully; neither of you will succeed by simply dashing off a sketchy collection of random thoughts. Perhaps the most important thing the sales representative does is anticipate the question, Why should I buy from you—I'm happy with my present supplier? You anticipate a similar question. Why should I buy your idea—we're doing OK?

Only when the sales representative has gathered and sorted all the facts and anticipated objections can the presentation be planned. He or she may even jot down the things to say to the customer and carefully rehearse the presentation. In your case, you will want to outline your report before you start to write.

The working outline prepared by the controller of Northwest Leather Goods, after going through several revisions, might appear as follows.

> Kick-off statement referring to previous conversations
> Introduction
> > Background
> > Purpose and Scope
> Advantages of Present System
> Arguments for Centralized Purchasing
> Cost versus Savings
> Recommendations
> Effective Date

Based on the final outline, the controller might produce the following report. Our comments appear at the right.

NORTHWEST LEATHER GOODS

Office Letter

To: Mr. J. William Hertz

From: C. R. Amend

Subject: Centralization of the
Purchasing Function

Date: February 16, 19--

I have mentioned to you several times recently that I think we
should consider centralizing the purchasing function in the
company. The following report represents my position.

INTRODUCTION

During the past year Northwest Leather Goods made purchases of
internal-use equipment and supplies amounting to more than
$380,000. The items purchased included computer equipment,
automobiles and trucks, furniture and furnishings, stationery,
calculators, books, typewriters, and dozens of other things
for company use. These purchases were made by 33 different
individuals in our twelve operating departments.

After careful study I have arrived at the conclusion that under
our present set-up we are spending more money than we should
to obtain the materials we need. Although there are certain
advantages to our present system--flexibility, primarily--it
can be extremely wasteful in a larger organization. For example,
selecting a dozen major purchases made last year, I compared
the prices of the suppliers selected with those offered by other
suppliers for similar (or better) products and found that in at
least seven instances we could have saved from 15 percent to
20 percent if we had made cost comparisons or obtained competitive bids.

A brief reference to previous conversations pulls aside the curtain for the report that follows.

The introduction establishes the background, telling the recipient why the report was written. Note that specific data has been supplied, a must in nearly all selling reports.

Mr. J. William Hertz
Page 2
February 16, 19--

Purpose and Scope

The purpose of this report is to propose a new system for
internal-use purchasing. The discussion that follows, including recommendations, is not intended to apply to purchasing for
manufacturing. The Manufacturing Division would continue to
purchase raw materials, equipment, and supplies used in the
production process.

ADVANTAGES OF DECENTRALIZED PURCHASING

There are some advantages to our present system of allowing
department managers and supervisors to do their own buying.
The buyers can tailor their purchases to their own specific
requirements, for one thing. Then, too, they may get faster,
more personalized service since there are no in-company channels
to go through.

Decentralized purchasing is perhaps the most effective way to
buy internal-use goods in a small enterprise. Indeed, it has
worked quite well at Northwest over the years. However, with
the dramatic growth in the company during the past five years
we can longer be classified as small. We now need a more sys-
tematic procedure for handling purchases.

ARGUMENTS FOR CENTRALIZED PURCHASING

There are five major reasons why I think we should consider
centralizing the purchasing function in Northwest Leather Goods:

1. If all purchases were made in a centralized department, we
    would buy in larger quantities instead of piecemeal. We
    would therefore get better prices, higher discounts, and
    lower transportation rates.

The purpose is specifically
stated, along with the scope,
or perimeters. It is important
to establish perimeters here;
otherwise, the reader may
jump to false conclusions.

Under the heading
ADVANTAGES OF
DECENTRALIZED
PURCHASING, Amend is
careful to acknowledge the
merits of the present system.
When recommending a new
procedure, try to find
something good to say about
the existing one. If you put
your reader on the defensive
(the president of Northwest
Leather Goods may be the
author of the present
system), you can easily lose
your case. Even though you
need to be critical of the
existing system if you are to
sell the idea for change, be
tactfully critical.

Arguments for centralized
purchasing are enumerated
and explained. Note,
however, that the writer has
avoided superlatives. The use
of *should* and *would* rather
than *will* make the statements
less dogmatic.

Mr. J. William Hertz
Page 3
February 16, 19--

2. Concentration of purchasing would allow us to hire special-
    ists--people who know the best sources of supply and the
    best time to buy. This know-how should enable us to get
    better quality at lower prices.

3. Centralization would lead to uniformity in purchasing pro-
    cedures and, at the same time, permit us to pinpoint
    responsibility for effective buying.

4. By centralizing purchasing, we would eliminate duplications
    in buying, overordering, unnecessary varieties, and inflated
    inventories.

5. Centralization would give us better control over what and
    how much we buy. Right now many people are authorized to
    contract for purchases (for which the company is liable),
    a situation which could be dangerous.

COST VERSUS SAVINGS

Assuming that Northwest Leather Goods will continue to make
annual purchases of at least $380,000 (the amount will undoubt-
edly be larger as the company grows), and assuming that we can
save a minimum of 15 percent of this amount by judicious buying,
the annual savings could be around $57,000. This figure does
not take into account the time of the purchasing people in the
various departments, who are required to do a good deal of
research to find the things they need.

We should be able to hire a purchasing manager for $20,000 to
$25,000 a year; an assistant for $15,000 to $18,000; and a
secretary for $11,000 to $13,000. Assuming the maximum in each
instance, the salary costs would be about $56,000 a year;
fringe benefits, about $20,000. I have assumed that office
space and equipment will cost no more than at present, in view
of the expenses now incurred in the various individual departments.

**Again, in proposing change,
the question of cost *must* be
discussed. And it deserves a
major head.**

Mr. J. William Hertz
Page 4
February 16, 19--

Although the savings of $57,000 versus $76,000 in payroll costs
would seem to make this a losing proposition, it should be
remembered that purchases will increase substantially, perhaps
dramatically, while personnel costs will remain relatively static.
But, more important, the hidden savings in better products that
will have a longer life, reduced inventories, elimination of
"waste" buying, etc., could be very substantial. I would estimate that these hidden savings could amount to $60,000 a year
or more.

Although the writer has engaged in speculation—which she must do—her arguments are soft-pedaled and convincing.

RECOMMENDATIONS

Based on the foregoing analysis, I recommend that we:

1. Establish a centralized purchasing department and assign
   to it all responsibility for all major internal-use pur-
   chases--that is, anything over $25.

2. Appoint a purchasing director--a person thoroughly trained
   and experienced in the purchasing function and preferably
   one who has special knowledge of mechanical and automated
   equipment. This individual would report directly to you
   or, if you prefer, to me.

3. Authorize the purchasing director to employ an assistant
   manager and one secretary.

Recommendations are specific rather than general.

EFFECTIVE DATE

If this proposal is accepted, I suggest an effective date of
July 1. This will give us time to find the right person for
the director's job, set up a tentative operational plan, and
issue the necessary instructions to the employees affected.

The suggestion of an effective date simply anticipates the president's likely question, When?

YOUR TURN

Assume that, at the request of the executive vice president of your company, R. J. Hillyer, you have completed a week's investigation of serious bottlenecks in the Shipping Department. The problem, which has existed for several weeks, has resulted in serious delays in getting out customer orders. Some customers have canceled their orders; others are angrily protesting. Your investigation shows that the problem is primarily people—specifically, the manager of the department and two supervisors. The turnover in Shipping personnel is extremely high, and there is general unrest among those remaining. Your talks with these people, as well as with some of those who have already left, indicate that their main complaint is constant harassment from the department's management staff.

Choose a title for your memorandum (subject); then write the opening paragraph and an introduction, which includes a reference to purpose and scope. Compare your work with that shown on pages 197-198.

HIGHLIGHTS OF CHAPTER 5

In writing selling reports:

1. Plan carefully; think through the entire situation before you start to write.
2. Gather all the facts and double-check them for accuracy and relevancy.
3. Anticipate objections and jot down ideas in response.
4. Prepare a detailed outline, and be prepared to change it as writing progresses.
5. Put yourself in the shoes of the recipient and try to imagine what materials in the report would be most convincing to you.
6. Edit every sentence and paragraph to make sure your meaning is clear.
7. Beware of exaggerating, stating opinions as facts, and using grossly biased statements.
8. Use tact and discretion.

CHAPTER 6

Form reports

Many routine reports are one- or two-page affairs that contain mainly figures and/or names and very little, if any, narrative. By "routine" we don't mean that such reports aren't important, but that they are prepared on some fixed schedule—daily, weekly, biweekly, monthly, etc.

If you are required to submit periodic reports, you will save time by designing forms for them. This makes the preparation a more or less clerical operation. Examples follow.

EXAMPLE 1: WEEKLY OVERTIME REPORT

Because overtime expense is of concern to the financial vice president of Claybaugh Inc., each department manager is required to report weekly the overtime hours worked by employees. The report covers not only the number of hours but the reason overtime was authorized.

On page 82 is the warehouse manager's report for the week of March 9. The form for this report was designed to save time.

Quick Analysis

1. The form is prepared on the typewriter and duplicated in quantity so that it becomes a fill-in job for each department manager. Everything in the form is duplicated except the name of the division, date, names of employees and hours worked, and narrative comments.

2. The form may be filled in by hand or on the typewriter. If by hand, the fill-in lines for division name, date, and comments are important. If the typewriter is used, the lines may be omitted.

3. The distribution list at the bottom shows who is receiving copies of the report. O'Neill, the name circled, is getting this particular copy.

4. No "covering" memo is required for most form reports. Usually they are enclosed in an interoffice envelope for distribution.

WEEKLY OVERTIME REPORT

Division Warehousing   Week of March 9   19 --

Employee	Unit	S	M	T	W	T	F	S	Total
Bradley	Receiving	6							6
Coryell	Warehousing		4	4			4		12
Hawley	Warehousing		4	4			2		10
Martin	Shipping			2	6			4	12
Stein	Inventory		2	2	2	2	2		10
Zachary	Receiving	6							6
Total Overtime		12	10	12	8	2	8	4	56

Comments: The two employees in Receiving handled a rail shipment that had to be unloaded Sunday to avoid demurrage charges.
Overtime in Warehousing was required to relocate the Damaged
Goods Received section. Martin, in Shipping, made ready three
special rush shipments to Trans-Export. A new inventory control system is being set up, which accounts for the overtime
hours in Inventory.

Distribution: Caulfield, Hernandez, O'Neill, Rice, Villiapano

EXAMPLE 2: ANNIVERSARY REMINDER

The top executives at McGibbon-Kittredge Corporation encourage department managers to acknowledge (usually by a congratulatory letter and perhaps a special luncheon or dinner) the anniversaries celebrated by their employees. So at the end of every month, the Personnel Relations Division sends a report to each manager showing anniversary dates coming up the following month.

The personnel relations manager designed the following form to routinize this situation.

Anniversary Reminder

To: Francis R. Buchanan

Date: May 24, 19--

Next month's anniversaries in your department are as follows:

Name	Years Employed	Anniversary Date
Karen Fremont	10	June 17
Arnold Glasser	10	June 7
W. T. Chu	5	June 1

Personnel Relations Division

Quick Analysis

This fill-in form is printed in "snap-out" sets. Only the addressee's name, the date, names of celebrants, years employed, and anniversary dates are entered.

EXAMPLE 3: COST VARIANCE ANALYSIS

In most companies, each department manager receives one or more financial reports periodically. One report shows the amount budgeted for each expense, the actual amount spent, and the difference (variance). A simple cost variance analysis follows.

```
                    COST VARIANCE ANALYSIS
           For the Month of  February          , 19 --
           Department         Advertising and Promotion
```

ACCOUNT	BUDGET AMOUNT	ACTUAL AMOUNT	VARIANCE (+ or -)
Salaries	55,800	66,200	+10,400
Overtime	2,900	1,100	- 1,800
Supplies Used	4,200	4,200	--
Telephone	2,200	2,600	+ 400
Postage	11,400	10,300	- 1,100
Travel	3,100	2,500	- 600
Miscellaneous	1,600	2,300	+ 700
Totals	81,200	89,200	+ 8,000

```
Distribution:  Powers, Katz, Olney, Villiers
                                  Prepared by _____
```

Quick Analysis

1. Only the date, department designation, amounts, and reporter's initials (or name) need to be supplied.
2. The $ sign is nearly always omitted in fill-in financial reports. It is understood that all figures are money amounts.
3. Generally, figures in financial reports are rounded off to the nearest $100.
4. The fill-in data on financial reports may be handwritten; generally, however, it is typewritten.

DESIGNING FILL-IN FORM REPORTS

Following are guidelines for designing fill-in form reports.

Size of Reports

Use a standard sheet—8½ by 11 inches is best. Not only is this size easy for the typist to use, it is also easier to file and retrieve from the file.

In some businesses, a half sheet (5½ by 8½ inches) is recommended for short reports because it saves paper; however, this saving may be canceled out by the inconvenience in filing and retrieving. In any event, avoid the small, offbeat sizes such as 5 by 3 or 8 by 4; not only are they hard to handle but they are easily lost.

Concise Headings

Give your report a name and display it prominently so that the reader can quickly see what it is about. The heading should be as brief as possible, yet specific. Compare:

Not: PERSONNEL REPORT
But: MONTHLY EMPLOYEE TURNOVER

Not: UNCOLLECTIBLE ACCOUNTS REPORT
But: QUARTERLY WRITE-OFF OF UNCOLLECTIBLE ACCOUNTS

Not: REPORT OF ORDERS PENDING AND NOT YET FILLED
But: BIWEEKLY REPORT OF UNFILLED ORDERS

Vertical Spacing

If the report is to be filled in by typewriter, make certain that the writing lines conform with the spacing of typewriter lines. This is very often overlooked by forms designers (and printers), and the typist is required to adjust the cylinder knob with each line entry.

If the form is to be filled in by hand, allow a minimum width of ¼ inch between lines.

Horizontal Spacing

Be sure there is plenty of room for each entry. This sounds like an unnecessary bit of advice, but lack of writing space is the biggest complaint of those who fill in forms—application blanks, credit forms, income tax blanks, etc. For example:

NOT

Employee Wilkinson, Mary Dept. Inv. C. Job Title Syst. An.

BUT

Employee Wilkinson, Mary Department Inventory Control Job Title Systems Analyst

NOT

Employee	Department	Hourly Rate	Hours Worked	Earnings
Birnbaum, C.	Manufacturing	$6.80	40	$272.00
Frankheimer, G.	Cust. Serv.	$8.60	38	288.80
McGeoghan, Mc.	Data Proc. Cont.	$9.20	40	368.00

BUT

Employee	Department	Hourly Rate	Hours Worked	Earnings
Birnbaum, C.	Manufacturing	$6.80	40	$272.00
Frankheimer, G.	Customer Services	$8.60	38	288.80
McGeoghan, Mc.	Data Processing Control	$9.20	40	368.00

Rulings for Distinction

You can give your fill-in forms distinction by varying the "weight" of the rulings. If you are having the form executed by a printer, use hairline rules for lines on which data is to be entered and heavier rules or double hairlines to separate zones or areas on the form. In the form illustrated, all three rules are used.

RETURNED PARTS SUMMARY   DATE:

SECTION NO.

TO: _____

PART NO. and NAME	QUANTITY	COST	
		UNIT	TOTAL

SIGNED _____   TOTAL EXPENSE

If you are having the form executed on a typewriter, use a single underscore for lines on which the data is to be entered and a double underscore to separate zones or areas on the form. Also try to use a special typewriter typeface for the captions and other words that are part of the standard form. In that way, the fill-ins that are later typed in on the form will stand out more clearly.

YOUR TURN

To conserve gas, Rheinhold Distributors encourages its sales representatives to cut car mileage as much as possible, using other forms of transportation when available. The marketing director has instructed each of the fifteen district-sales office managers to submit a monthly report, showing the miles driven by each representative that month, the miles driven the previous month, and the + or − variance. (Each + variance is to be explained in a special section provided on the form.) The miles driven by all representatives during the present and previous month are to be totaled, along with the + and − variances. The person preparing the report is to identify himself/herself at the bottom of the form.

Design the form, using whatever rulings you think are appropriate; then check your results with the form on page 198.

EXAMPLE 4: A NARRATIVE FORM REPORT

Some periodic reports are narrative rather than fill-in. Even so, they often lend themselves to a standard format that can be used over and over. An example is a company's monthly operations report, which include a comparison of performance with the same month a year ago and a recap of the current year to date.

Following is the format developed by the controller of Banner Electronics for the monthly operations report.

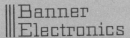
Banner
Electronics

Results of June 19-- Operations

OVERALL COMPANY PERFORMANCE IN JUNE

Revenue   Operations in June produced a total revenue of $2,835,000, which was $220,000 over budget.

Income   Net operating income (NOI) was $433,000, over budget by $171,000.

Expenses Expenses for the month were generally in line with budget, the exceptions being manufacturing, advertising, factory wages, and dealer services. These exceptions are referred to later.

Last Year Compared with June of last year, we had a sales increase of $471,000 and an NOI increase of $139,500--5.3 percent higher as a percent of sales.

YEAR-TO-DATE COMPANY PERFORMANCE

For the first six months (January-June), the company is over revenue budget by $287,000 and ahead of last year by $573,000. NOI for this period is $440,000 over budget and $817,000 over last year.

TELEVISION DIVISION RESULTS IN JUNE

Revenue   Revenue in June amounted to $1,410,000, or $127,500 over budget. General Sales contributed $99,000 to the increase, and Contracts contributed $28,500.

Income   NOI was $263,000, or $126,000 over budget.

Since this is a narrative commentary accompanying an operating statement, this simple title is sufficient.

The general summary of operations is presented first. This may be all that some readers will want to see; thus it is better at the beginning than at the end.

The side headings—Revenue, Income, Expenses, and Last Year—stand out. Many people find financial analyses dull and hard to assimilate. For them, frequent headings are extremely valuable.

A year-to-date recap provides a broader perspective of company performance.

2

Expenses   All expenses were in line with budget. Pro-
             vision for uncollectible contracts reflects
             the monthly adjustment necessary to amortize
             the deferred expense that was created at the
             end of last year. Manufacturing costs appear
             high in relation to budget; however, it is
             anticipated that a reasonable adjustment will
             be made as a result of a physical inventory on
             June 27. The physical inventory provides the
             basis for transfer to a perpetual system.

AUDIO SYSTEMS DIVISION RESULTS IN JUNE

Revenue   Revenue in June amounted to $1,425,000, which
             exceeded budget by $51,500 and last year by
             $243,900. This can be attributed to growing
             interest of consumers in sophisticated tape
             and record installations.

Income   NOI was $169,500, or $71,000 over budget.

Expenses   June expenses were well in line with budget.
             Although advertising, factory wages, and dealer
             services were well over budget, reductions in
             manufacturing, research, and administrative
             expenses made the total expenses just about
             even with budget.

REMAINDER OF THE YEAR

The next six months appear to be very favorable, according to
departmental reports. Two new contracts are in the offing--one
in automobile manufacturing and another in retail distribution.
If these come in, we expect additional sales of from $300,000
to $500,000 in new business from these sources alone. Unusually
heavy expenses are anticipated, however, in inventory adjustments

**A look ahead is a fitting
ending for this report,
anticipating top
management's sure-to-be-
asked question, How do
things look for the rest of the
year?**

3

as well as in factory renovations and relocations. In any
event, all predictions are for an overall increase in revenue
of 20 percent over last year and an NOI rate of 12 percent.

Morris R. Nagle

Morris R. Nagle
Controller

HIGHLIGHTS OF CHAPTER 6

In designing forms for periodic reports, keep the following in mind:

1. Give the form a name and display it prominently. The title should be as brief as possible but specific enough to identify the contents of the report.
2. Use standard-size paper, such as 8½ by 11 inches. This size is easy for the typist as well as the file clerk to handle.
3. Design the form so that the least number of fill-ins is required.
4. If the report is to be filled in by typewriter, horizontal rules may be omitted. However, where they are used, make sure they conform to typewriter spacing.
5. If the report is to be filled in by hand, horizontal rules are important. Allow a minimum of ¼ inch between lines.
6. Allow plenty of room for each entry; too often fill-in space is inadequate, which results in unintelligible abbreviations.
7. In financial reports, the $ sign is nearly always omitted, and money amounts are rounded off to the nearest $100.
8. You can give the form distinction by varying the weight of the rulings.

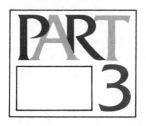

PART 3

Formally structured reports

Some writers prefer a more formal structure than the memorandum for their reports. Generally, but not always, these reports are a little longer than a typical memorandum and are likely to be about things of more than ordinary importance. Moreover, the writing style is often less personal than in memorandums.

Yet these distinctions are arbitrary. There is no reason why a formally structured report has to be long or impersonal or weighty in subject matter. The only *real* distinction between a memorandum and a formally structured report is the first page. Some reporters just happen to think that a report written on plain paper is more businesslike and important than one written on memo stationery.

In this section, we focus on achieving emphasis in your writing and using display effectively. These techniques are, of course, equally applicable to informal memorandums.

CHAPTER 7

Parts and setup of formally structured reports

The number of parts in a formally structured report varies. There is no set rule—everything depends on the type of report you are writing. If you write a report in which you analyze a problem and present your recommendations, the report may have five parts as follows:

TITLE

INTRODUCTION

BODY

SUMMARY

CONCLUSIONS AND RECOMMENDATIONS

Report Title

Needless to say, every report needs a title. In some reports, the writer provides a title page and also repeats the title on the first page of the report itself. You'll want to keep the title as brief as possible, but when you find it hard to keep it to one line, you can use a subtitle. For example:

EQUIPMENT REPLACEMENT ANALYSIS
An Evaluation of Equipment as a Capital Investment

Introduction

The first part of a formally structured report is usually the introduction. It often covers the following points, although not necessarily in the order listed.

History or background

Purpose

Need

Method

Scope

Definition of terms

History or Background.   It may be desirable to preface the report with a brief history or background, which describes the events leading up to the present situation. Whether or not you need this material will depend on the subject of the report. If, for example, you are proposing a new image for your company because the public's concept of it is out of date, you may want to trace the history of the organization to show how its present image developed.

Purpose.   From the background or historical information, you can proceed to state the purpose of your report. If no background information is needed, the purpose will probably be the first thing in your report. Of course, it is one of the most important elements. You will remember that in informal memorandums the purpose may be understood, in which case a simple reference should be made to a written request or a meeting. In formally structured reports, however, the purpose is specifically stated (often under the heading *Purpose*).

Need.   Need refers to the writer's justification for the report. If, for example, you are proposing that the inventory control system be computerized, you may want to say why the present manual system is inadequate. For example, it takes too long to get a total picture of inventory status, and when you get it, the information is not accurate. This often results in delayed shipments to customers as well as inaccurate financial reports. And so on. You will find an example of the statement of need in the report on page 00.

Method.   Method refers to how you went about gathering the material for your report. In this chapter, you will see a report in which the writer found that a good deal of money is being wasted because the company is saturated with rarely used forms. Those reading the report (some of whom may be inflicted with the dread disease "form-itis") will want to know how the writer went about gathering the information. By describing the method, the writer routs the notion some readers may have that he or she is merely guessing.

Scope.   Scope, you may remember, refers to the perimeters of your report. Earlier, you saw a report in which the controller recommended a centralized purchasing set-up for the company. The controller was careful, however, to mention that it was not her intention that this new department would buy anything but internal-use goods, quieting the nerves of the Manufacturing Department staff who might have jumped to other conclusions.

Definition of Terms.   This subject is closely related to scope, but in some reports it has to be dealt with separately. Let's say you have been asked to make a microfilm survey in your company, recommending whether the company should do its own filming and developing or contract the job to outside agencies. As an expert in microfilming, you are likely to use terms that some of your readers aren't familiar with—microfilm, microfiche, planetary camera, rotary camera, film processing, and so on. You will want to define these terms early so that your readers will know what you're talking about.

Body of the Report

The body is, of course, the main part of the report. The material obviously will vary according to what you're writing about. In the report on pages 00-00, the body consists of everything under the headings ADVANTAGES OF DECENTRALIZED PUR-CHASING, ARGUMENTS FOR CENTRALIZED PURCHASING, and COST VERSUS SAVINGS.

Summary or Synopsis

In reports that are somewhat long and complicated, it is often a good idea to prepare a summary or synopsis, which is a condensation of the main points covered in the body of the report. These main points may be given headings, followed by enumerations, or they may be written as a brief narrative statement, thus:

SUMMARY

In this study the author learned that Swiftmour Inc. ranks well below the median in the industry in such employee benefits as retirement programs, insurance and hospitalization, profit sharing, stock-purchase plans, and vacation policies. Indeed, of the 100 companies studied, 67 lead Swiftmour in these areas. On the other hand, Swiftmour ranks slightly above the median in expenditures for education and training, salaries, incentive compensation, and employee services.

Traditionally, the summary has been placed at the end of the report. However, there is a trend toward moving it up front, either just before or after the introduction. This makes it easy for people in a hurry to get the gist of the author's findings without having to wade through the entire report.

Some writers prepare a brief summary at the end of each major section, much like those you have seen at the ends of chapters in textbooks. This is helpful in reports that contain a great deal of data that is difficult to remember from a quick reading. However, these interspersed summaries do not eliminate the need for a complete summary at the beginning or end of the report.

Conclusions and Recommendations

In most fact-finding reports, the author is expected to include a statement of the conclusions drawn from the study, along with specific recommendations for action. These may be combined, thus:

Conclusions and Recommendations

Based on the findings of this study, the following conclusions and recommendations are offered.

1. Increased Mileage Allowance. With the increasing cost of automobile owner-ship—purchase price, operating costs, and maintenance—the present allowance of 18¢ per mile appears to be inadequate. It is recommended that a new minimum allowance of 25¢ a mile be established immediately, along with a plan for increasing this rate as costs increase.
2. Additional Field Supervisors. As the sales organization grows, . . .

As with the summary, there is a trend toward placing conclusions and recommendations at the front of the report, usually following the summary. However, more and more writers incorporate conclusions and recommendations into the summary.

ABOUT THE PARTS OF A REPORT

Talking about the parts of a report is comparable to talking about cooking. Your favorite recipe for chili will look nothing like the one for lasagna or mulligatawny soup. Thus it is with a report; a quarterly financial report won't resemble one recommending a change in the marketing mix. You have to keep your readers in mind and select the parts—and the sequence in which they appear—so that readers can quickly and fully understand your message.

A SAMPLE FORMALLY STRUCTURED REPORT

Now let's look at a typical formally structured report. Here is the situation. Babbitt-Thompson Corporation, like most large companies, conducts much of its business on paper. Recently, a new unit was added to the Data Processing Division—called the Systems Unit. The new systems manager is to study ways of reducing costs and increasing effectiveness through continuing analysis of systems and methods.

"One of the first things I want you to do," the new manager was told by his boss, "is to make a thorough analysis of the forms used in the company. I suspect we are wasting thousands of dollars on unnecessary paperwork. Take whatever time you need, but I want a complete report, including your recommendations."

The report follows, including our commentary.

FORM USAGE IN BABBITT-THOMPSON CORPORATION

Prepared by

Philip R. Santini
Manager, Systems Unit

for

R. H. Bixby, Treasurer

November 9, 19--

There are many ways to set
up a title page, and this is but
one example. It usually shows
the title of the report, the
writer's name, the name of
the person who asked for the
report, and the date.

FORM USAGE IN BABBITT-THOMPSON CORPORATION

INTRODUCTION

Nearly every organization of any size eventually runs up against what is commonly called "the forms problem." That is, for a number of years the various forms used in conducting company business are allowed to proliferate, with little or no attention to need, quantity, and cost. Suddenly there is an awareness--prompted by mounting clerical costs, printing expenses, and bulging files--of the need to take a hard look at the number of forms in use, why and how they are used, and cost.

This is the situation in Babbitt-Thompson--and it is not an unusual one. The general area of form usage is more often ignored than confronted. This study, made at the request of Treasurer R. H. Bixby, is the result of this company's determination to "confront" rather than ignore.

Definitions

The term form refers to every piece of paper that contains information--whether printed, mimeographed, hectographed, or photocopied--with blanks on which data is to be entered. Specifically, the following are included in this definition:

1. Numbered forms (invoices, purchase orders, checks, etc.)
2. Unnumbered forms (stock reports, sales summaries, etc.)
3. Single sheets and cards
4. Sets of sheets and cards (i.e., two or more)
5. Forms bound in books (fixed asset records, for example)
6. Letterheads and envelopes (including memorandums)
7. Form letters

Even though the report has a separate title page, the title is repeated on the first page of the report itself.

The introduction (which may also be called background or problem) includes a statement that justifies the report, the purpose, and other information such as definitions of terms to prevent misunderstanding, scope, and procedure (or method) used in gathering the information. The material under the first main heading will vary from one report to another.

2

8. Routing slips, telephone message blanks, etc.
9. Continuous and snap-out forms
10. Forms used in connection with data processing (punched cards and printouts, for example)

Scope

The author has limited his investigation to a general consideration of the number of forms now in use, the quantities required, and the probable cost. There was no attempt to make a complete analysis of need for a particular form, forms design, methods of preparation, equipment required, and effect on interdepartmental procedures. It is assumed that these matters will be thoroughly researched at the appropriate time, as recommended later in this report.

Sometimes it is important to tell what the report does *not* cover as well as what it *does* cover. This delimitation usually comes under the heading *Scope.*

Procedure

In gathering the information for this report, the writer:

1. Collected copies of all the forms used in the company. This was done by memorandum in which all department heads were asked to submit five copies of every form used--whether it originated in that department or was received from another source.

When all the forms were collected, they were tallied on a survey sheet, thus:

In this report it is important for readers to know how the information was obtained. The heading may be *Procedure* or *Method.*

Forms Survey

Name of Form	No. of Copies	How Prepared	How Often Prepared	How Long Retained	Departments Affected
Receiving Report	3	Hand	Daily	Indef.	Inventory, Accounting, Sales

3

    2.   Interviewed 160 employees concerning the origin of new forms, the value of the forms used, and the disposition of forms.

    3.   Examined in a cursory manner the design, size, and general purpose and content of each form.

    4.   Determined the interdepartmental flow of each form.

    5.   Inspected all forms with similar titles and purposes for overlapping of information.

    6.   Traced the disposition of each form (transmittal, file, destruction, etc.)

    7.   Made a rough estimate of the cost of each form in terms of clerical time, printing, and disposition.

FINDINGS

Usage Quantities

    A total of 497 forms are now in use in Babbitt-Thompson. The following table shows usage quantities.

The body begins here.

USAGE QUANTITIES OF BABBITT-THOMPSON FORMS

Annual Usage	No. of Forms	% of Forms	Individual Copies*	% of Copies	Cumulative % of Copies
1-200	320	64.4	57,300	6.1	6.1
201-400	61	12.3	45,200	4.7	10.8
401-2000	70	14.1	190,300	21.0	31.8
2001-4000	25	5.0	162,400	17.0	48.8
4001-20,000	17	3.4	305,800	32.2	81.0
20,001-40,000	2	0.4	104,000	10.9	90.9
Over 40,000	2	0.4	81,000	8.1	100.0
	497	100.0	946,000	100.0	100.0

    *These figures represent copies of forms, some of which are single and others in sets (duplicate, triplicate, etc.).

4

As will be seen by the preceding table, nearly 65 percent of the company's forms are used in annual quantities of 200 or less; moreover, they account for only about 6 percent of the total number of pieces of paper. It must be remembered, however, that low-usage forms are generally those that are not prepared by mechanical methods and thus require more clerical time than high-usage forms.

At present there is no restriction on developing new forms and duplicating them in quantity. Nor are there restrictions on format, number of copies made, and distribution.

During the past year alone, 70 new forms were introduced, 50 of which duplicate information on other forms. So far as can be determined, no forms were discontinued.

Few people in Babbitt-Thompson have any idea how many forms are now in use, including department heads and other executives. About 75 percent of the people questioned guessed that there were "about 100."

At least 50 percent of the clerical employees who deal with the forms have erroneous ideas as to the origin of the form, its value, and its ultimate disposition.

Reproduction

A wide variety of printing processes are used to reproduce forms, including photocopy, mimeograph, hectograph (Ditto), multilith, letterpress, handmade, etc. Where forms are printed commercially, eight different suppliers are used. Costs vary widely. For example, in four instances one supplier's costs were almost double those of another for nearly identical work.

Photocopying is a very popular method of reproduction, even where several hundred copies may be required of a particular form. This is extremely costly when compared with mimeographing and similar reproduction methods.

Complete accuracy is mandatory in reports. If you aren't sure, say so. Note: "*So far as can be determined,* no forms were discontinued."

5

Numbering

Except for a very few forms (sales tickets and purchase orders, for example), numbers are not assigned to forms. This makes it extremely difficult to identify the subject and the source.

Consolidation

Although no attempt was made to analyze all forms in terms of the possibilities of consolidation, a cursory examination revealed a large number of opportunities. For example, of the 34 different forms used in the Personnel Division, at least 10 could easily be eliminated by combining them with others. In a recent study, one large company was able to "boil down" 468 separate forms into 98 (as many as 12 forms were consolidated into a single form) and calculated its savings in many thousands of dollars.

Cost

Although the cost of reproducing the 497 forms used in Babbitt-Thompson cannot be precisely determined, a rough estimate (including photocopying) is $15,000 annually.

The real cost of forms, however, can be measured only in terms of the clerical payroll--that is, the actual time that people spend working with the forms: reading, filling in, processing, transmitting, filing, etc. Authorities in forms design and control say that for every dollar of reproduction expense $25 is spent on clerical operations. This would mean that forms are costing Babbitt-Thompson $375,000 to $400,00 a year, assuming the $15,000 estimate of reproduction cost is valid.

If the company were able to reduce forms expense by, say, 20 percent (a conservative estimate, in the writer's opinion), the annual savings could be from $75,000 to $80,000. This

Do not make claims that you cannot support. Note: "Although no attempt was made to analyze all forms in terms of the possibilities of consolidation, a cursory examination revealed . . ."

6

saving would, of course, be cumulative and over a long period
would be much, much greater.

Effect on Systems and Procedures

Fully as important as cost of the forms is their effect
on systems and procedures in an enterprise. Although a form
is only a piece of paper, it often dictates procedure. Thus
the "medium becomes the message"; that is, form content can
determine how hundreds of employees spend their time, the work
flow not only within a single department but among any number
of departments, equipment requirements, and so on. From the
writer's brief analysis, this fact would seem to have particular
relevance in Babbitt-Thompson. Anything that can be done to
eliminate or combine forms, to simplify their design or mechanize
their preparation will have an effect that reaches well beyond
the form itself.

Disposition

At present there is no standard system for disposing of
forms that are no longer needed. The result is that company
files are bulging with forms that are of no value, and every
year additional filing equipment is purchased to house these
records. Moreover, duplicate files are found throughout the
company; that is, three separate divisions may retain the same
records (and retain them indefinitely). This is expensive not
only in clerical time but also in equipment and space requirements.

Some records must be retained for specific periods, federal,
state, and local regulations require it. So far as can be determined, these records have not been specifically identified in
Babbitt-Thompson.

**Don't reach specific
conclusions based on flimsy
evidence. Note the "hedging"
statement: "From the writer's
brief analysis, this fact *would
seem* to have . . ."**

**Observe the clear writing—
no wasted words, good
transition between sentences
to lead the reader from one
thought to the next, simple
words.**

7

RECOMMENDATIONS

Based on this brief study, the writer has a strong convic-
tion that a great deal of money is being wasted on forms in
Babbitt-Thompson, not only in reproduction costs but in the
time of employees, investment in equipment, and procedural "red
tape." It is therefore recommended that:

1. A forms control program be established in Babbitt-Thompson
   for the purpose of:

   a. Eliminating all unnecessary forms.
   b. Controlling the number of new forms introduced in the
      company.
   c. Consolidating all the forms used in the company that
      have the same purpose.
   d. Redesigning forms to reduce clerical time and clerical
      error.
   e. Controlling the methods used for forms reproduction in
      order to select the most efficient process.
   f. Limiting the distribution of forms to those who are
      actually affected by the information on them.

2. The company employ a supervisor of forms control, with the
   full-time responsibility for establishing physical and
   functional standards, assisting department heads and others
   in designing forms, supervising the printing and other
   duplication, and establishing a retention and disposition
   policy. This supervisor would, it seems logical, report
   to the manager of the Systems Unit.

3. A functional forms index be set up, which would contain all
   forms grouped according to the purpose they service.

4. A Forms Standardization Committee be appointed, made up of
   one representative from each operating division. This would
   be a standing committee, which would approve all proposed
   new forms before they are released for reproduction.

Bixby, the treasurer, asked for the writer's recommendations. This report would be of very little value without them.

Recommendations are usually numbered so that they are easy to refer to when the report is discussed.

The writer's recommendations are specific and complete. They may not all be accepted, but they leave no doubt that he did his homework.

5. A standard retention-disposition policy be established, to make certain that valuable records (from a historical as well as a legal standpoint) are retained and to provide for destruction of records that are no longer of value.

BINDING AND TRANSMITTAL

The report illustrated may be stapled (two or three staples placed vertically on the left side) or it may be placed inside a heavy-paper binder.

Such reports are usually transmitted by a memorandum, which may be paper-clipped to the stapled report or to the binder. (Some reporters bind it in with the report, in which case it is the first page.)

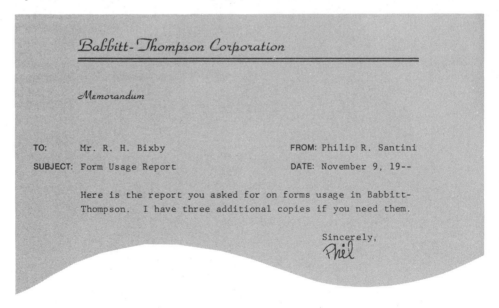

Babbitt-Thompson Corporation

Memorandum

TO: Mr. R. H. Bixby   FROM: Philip R. Santini
SUBJECT: Form Usage Report   DATE: November 9, 19--

Here is the report you asked for on forms usage in Babbitt-Thompson. I have three additional copies if you need them.

Sincerely,
Phil

HIGHLIGHTS OF CHAPTER 7

1. Formally structured reports that analyze a problem and present recommendations generally have five parts: title, introduction, body, summary, and conclusions and recommendations.

a. The title should be as brief as possible, yet entirely clear. If you can't keep the title to one line, you can use a subtitle.

b. The introduction covers the following points (although not necessarily in the order listed): history or background, purpose, need, method, scope, and definition of terms.

c. The body is the main part of the report. In long reports it is very important to break up body copy with frequent side headings.

d. The summary contains the highlights of the report. It may be placed either at the end of the report or directly after the introduction.

e. Conclusions and recommendations may be combined, although they are often separated. The material may be placed at the end of the report or at the front, following the summary.

2. The formally structured report is usually stapled at the sides or placed inside a heavy-paper binder.

3. Formally structured reports are usually transmitted by memorandum, which may be:

a. Paper-clipped to the stapled report or binder or

b. Bound inside the report as page one.

Achieving emphasis

When you write business reports, you want to save the time and effort of your readers. This means, of course, choosing words they will understand and structuring your sentences and paragraphs in such a way that your readers can easily stay with you.

Also vital in good report writing is *emphasis*—accentuating the important ideas, facts, and concepts so that your reader quickly grasps those things that are most significant. Some of the most important ways of achieving emphasis are discussed in this chapter.

EMPHASIS IN SENTENCES AND PARAGRAPHS

You will be a more forceful writer if you compose your sentences and paragraphs so that your main ideas don't get buried in a maze of verbiage. Watch particularly the way in which you begin your sentences.

Variety in Sentence Openings

Vary the way in which you begin your sentences and paragraphs. Some writers tend to start every paragraph the same way. They particularly overwork *I, We, It,* and *There.* This does not mean that you should always avoid these words. You can't. But several *I, We,* and *It* openings in a row can produce monotony.

***There* and *It* Openings.** Especially to be avoided are too many *There* and *It* sentence openings, for these expletives tend to produce dull writing and weaken your emphasis. For example:

WEAK

There is a good deal of concern among union employees about the piecework compensation plan.

STRONGER

Union employees are greatly concerned about the piecework compensation plan.

WEAK

It is the recommendation of the Finance Committee that major capital expenditures be delayed for six months.

STRONGER

The Finance Committee recommends that major capital expenditures be delayed six months.

Prepositional Openings.   Watch for too many opening phrases that begin with *In, After, Upon,* and other prepositions. For example:

WEAK

In response to the company attorney's statement that letters are actually contracts and therefore should be approved by the Legal Department, I would say that this is appropriate in a limited number of situations.

STRONGER

The company attorney's recommendation, namely, that because letters are actually contracts they should be approved by the Legal Department, has limited application.

WEAK

After testing the first ad in six metropolitan dailies, we arrived at the conclusion that . . .

STRONGER

The results of the test ad in six metropolitan dailies led us to believe that . . .

WEAK

Upon making an analysis of production in January as compared with January of last year, we discovered that there was an increase rather than a decrease.

STRONGER

Production in January of this year, we discovered, actually increased over January of last year.

"Ing" Openings.   Often "ing" words as openers—*believing, knowing, considering,* etc.—signal a long wind-up before the pitch. For example:

WEAK

Knowing that Bates has always been slow about paying his bills but that he always eventually settles his account, we extended him a new line of credit.

STRONGER

We gave Bates a new line of credit, for even though he has always been slow about paying his bills, he eventually settles his account.

WEAK

Believing that we should include one major southern city in test-marketing the new Womblies, we chose Birmingham.

STRONGER

We chose Birmingham as a representative, major, southern city in which to test-market the new Womblies.

WEAK

Considering the difficulties under which Miss Clavell worked to gather this information, we think she did a remarkably good job.

STRONGER

Miss Clavell did a remarkably good job gathering this information, even though she worked under many difficulties.

Your Turn

Rewrite the following sentence, avoiding the "ing" opening. You will find a suggested rewrite on page 198.

Attempting to solve the problem of traffic jams in early morning and late afternoon, the personnel director suggested that the company stagger the beginning and closing times.

Positioning Main Thoughts

You can achieve emphasis by the position you give your main thoughts. Don't bury your important points in the middle of a sentence—put them in a primary position, either at the beginning of the sentence or at the end, or both. Here are examples.

MAIN IDEA BURIED

She resides in Eutaw Village and commutes to her job as vice president of Moroney Products Company.

MAIN IDEA UP FRONT

She is vice president of Moroney Products Company and commutes to work from her home in Eutaw Village.

MAIN IDEA BURIED

Professor Kincaid, in a speech before the International Training Directors Association convention, which was held in Toronto in July, stressed the importance of participative management.

MAIN IDEA UP FRONT

Professor Kincaid stressed the importance of participative management in a speech before the International Training Directors Association convention, which was held in Toronto in July.

MAIN IDEAS BURIED

With Watson's education and long experience in marketing management, it stands to reason that he would not be satisfied very long as a field troubleshooter, which we realized too late and lost him to Clauson's because he was overqualified for the position here.

MAIN IDEAS AT THE BEGINNING AND END

There is no doubt that Watson was overqualified. With his education and long experience in marketing management, it stands to reason that he would not be satisfied very long as a field troubleshooter. Unfortunately, we realized this too late and Clauson's hired him away from us.

Word Economy

We mentioned earlier the importance of removing deadwood from your writing in order to make your reports more readable. Deadwood also destroys emphasis. Here are examples.

DEADWOOD

With reference to the suggestion that we consider developing a new logo for Mainstream Inc., there are many reasons for doing so at this time.

SHARPER

A new logo for Mainstream Inc. is very desirable for several reasons.

DEADWOOD

Recognizing that this is an awkward time to try to install a new inventory control system, we recommend that the idea be given further study in the early part of next year.

SHARPER

A new inventory control system, although not feasible now, should be considered early next year.

Question Sentences

An occasional question can provide emphasis. For example:

What, then, is the role of forecasting in management control? The answer is simply this: to help determine whether and to what degree the long-range goals of the company can be accomplished.

Is acquisition the only way of achieving growth? Obviously not. However, it is the quickest way.

What do employees think about music in the office? Opinions vary a good deal, depending on where the employee is situated and the type of work he or she performs.

Repetition of Key Points

Another way of achieving emphasis of important points is by means of repetition.

Berkemier estimates that in a ten-year period we will save about $1,000,000 by putting our payroll on the computer. A million dollars! The figure boggles the mind.

Effective personnel administration means using human resources effectively. It means establishing productive relationships among employees. And it means developing people to reach their full potential. Effective personnel administration, then, is everybody's job.

But beware of repetition of words in the same sentence that, although spelled the same way, have different meanings:

Our financial interest will be protected only if every supervisor exhibits interest in cutting costs.

In typing business letters, our secretaries should be instructed to follow the style manual to the letter.

Record only those figures that are important to have on record.

Short Sentences

As mentioned earlier, an occasional short sentence provides strong emphasis. For example:

Carlsen insisted that MarCal offers discounts that are 10 to 20 percent higher than we offer him. Is he exaggerating? Perhaps. But again, perhaps not.

On the other hand, a leasing plan puts us in the automobile business, and we have always said we don't want that. Yet there are many advantages to leasing that are hard to ignore. Cost, for one.

Short Paragraphs

An occasional short paragraph can give very effective emphasis to an important idea or concept. For example:

In our attempts to improve our correspondence with stockholders, we should not overlook the importance of giving each correspondent the personal responsibility for managing his or her own "enterprise." The problem, according to exit interviews, is *oversupervision.*

In other words, people write better letters when they feel personally responsible for the results.

A few years ago the American Telephone and Telegraph Company made an exhaustive study of the problem of stockholder relations. This study revealed some startling results, and some of the findings are particularly relevant to our own problem in Synthrax . . .

THE COLON AND EXCLAMATION POINT

The colon and the exclamation point are devices that may be used to gain emphasis.

The Colon

Following are examples of the use of the colon for emphasis.

In fact, all methods improvement programs, no matter how they operate, have one objective in common: to save money.

Leased delivery equipment has one serious weakness: inflexibility. By inflexibility we mean that . . .

So there is no argument about whether we need better publicity and PR in Graham Inc. The question is simply this: Who? Obviously, if there is to be intelligent management of a publicity and PR effort, one person must be assigned the responsibility.

The Exclamation Point

The exclamation point is a "shout" that demands the reader's attention. It should, however, be used very sparingly.

We had counted on about 300 people at the Open House. Imagine our surprise when we registered our 500th guest!

This is not to say that this new policy solves all our problems. Far from it! Yet it will go a long way to ease the tension between the two departments.

According to the sales representative from OfficeMate, a typewriting speed of 100 words a minute (!) is not uncommon with this new model.

UNDERLINING AND CAPITALIZING

You can use the standard devices of underlining and capitalizing to emphasize important words and phrases. For example:

Certainly we ought to do everything possible to reduce the cost of letter writing, but let's not forget that the really important consideration is <u>results.</u> A letter that costs $5 to put in the mail may be very inexpensive if it obtains a $50,000 order.

There is only one answer to the question whether this is the right time to enter the Latin American market. And that answer is a definite NO.

It seems clear, then, that the issue is not quality <u>versus</u> economy but quality AND economy.

Again, be cautious about the use of these devices for achieving emphasis. Remember that striving too hard for emphasis usually results in no emphasis at all.

YOUR TURN

1. Rewrite the following sentence, putting the main idea up front. A suggested rewrite is on page 198.

The fact that employees find it difficult to deal objectively with sacred cows or in fact to remedy existing procedural bottlenecks makes the use of outside consultants in methods improvement highly attractive.

2. Edit the following, removing the deadwood. (See page 198 for a suggested solution.)

The basic underlying function of the accounts payable procedure is to maintain and provide a complete and accurate record of the amounts owed by the company to the various creditors of the firm and to make payment to the creditors when payment is due.

HIGHLIGHTS OF CHAPTER 8

1. Make your opening statements strong. (See the rewrite on pages 198-199.)

   Checkup. Substitute a different opening for each of the following.

   a. In offering credit, the principal purpose is to increase sales.
   b. There were six members present at the Suggestion Committee meeting.
   c. It is standard policy to give new employees one week's vacation the first year.
   d. After looking at the five marketing channels we now use, I have decided that two of them can be eliminated.
   e. Upon discovering that our present liability insurance is inadequate, the company attorney recommended additional coverage.
   f. Feeling that the piece-rate wage plan is unfair, the Manufacturing Committee proposed a complete revision.

2. Don't bury your most important ideas.

   Checkup. Rearrange the following sentences so that the main idea comes first. (See the suggested rewrite on page 199.)

a. The difference between the cost and the original price of the merchandise, regardless of the price at which the merchandise is sold, is called the initial mark-on.

b. The president, merchandise managers, chief accountant, treasurer, and director of personnel should be among the members of the Budget Committee.

c. For overseas personnel, especially those who come in close contact with foreign nationals, no part of the orientation program is as important as language training.

3. Don't destroy your emphasis by overwriting.

Checkup. Edit the following so that the ideas stand out more clearly. Use as many sentences as you think necessary. (See the suggested rewrite on page 199.)

It is the opinion of many that high-speed computing equipment is not absolutely essential for operations research studies, since exceedingly useful results have been obtained solely with mathematical techniques, without a computer, yet there is no denying the fact that computers reduce the man-hours required to solve formulas, develop data, and offer greater exploration of data to determine existing relationships.

4. Use occasional "question" sentences for emphasis.

Checkup. Use a question to introduce the following; then rewrite, using as many sentences as you need. (See the suggested rewrite on page 199.)

If an R&D operation is established, it might logically be located within any number of departments—Finance, Marketing, Product Planning, Research, Manufacturing, and so on, but it is my opinion that its manager should report directly to the president.

5. Use short sentences occasionally to achieve emphasis.

Checkup. Employ the technique of short sentences to give emphasis to the following. (See the suggested rewrite on page 199.)

In developing a company employee handbook, special attention must be given to such things as brevity, simplicity, photography, and cartoons.

6. Use a colon occasionally for emphasis.

Checkup. Rewrite the following, using a colon for emphasis. (See the suggested rewrite on page 199.)

In the evaluation of a suggestion system, it is important to understand that employees are not primarily motivated to make suggestions for monetary rewards but primarily to contribute their ideas to management.

7. Use an exclamation point (sparingly) for emphasis.

Checkup. Use an exclamation point in the following for emphasis. (See the suggested rewrite on page 199.)

When caught carrying canned hams to their cars, the two warehouse workers said they understood that the company expected employees to help themselves.

Using display effectively

NUMBERS IN REPORTS

Although numbers are essential in many business reports, the fact is that many readers are bewildered by them. Given a choice, most people would probably prefer to bypass statistical data than try to analyze and understand it. Following are four guidelines for using numbers in general (nonfinancial) reports.

Use Figures Sparingly

Make sure that figures are really necessary to a clear understanding of your message before you decide to include them. Obviously, in many interoffice communications you can't avoid numbers entirely—financial statement analysis, for example. On the other hand, you will need very few (if any) figures in dealing with, say, a plan for improving customer relations.

Separate Figures from Narrative

When possible, isolate statistical data from the narrative. Figures that are combined with words make for hard reading; so when you can, set them up in table form. Compare:

NARRATIVE

Anticipated savings in the Purchasing Department are $4000, or 9 percent; in the Credit Department, $2500, or 11 percent; in the Personnel Department, $6000, or 7½ percent; in the Manufacturing Department, $9000, or 9 percent; in the Finance Department, $3000, or 6 percent; in General Administrative, $1500, or 5 percent; and in the Marketing Department, $7500, or 12¼ percent.

TABLE FORM

The anticipated savings from this new mechanized system are shown in the following table.

Anticipated Savings by Department

Department	Savings ($)	Percent (%)
Purchasing	4000	9
Credit	2500	11
Personnel	6000	$7\frac{1}{2}$
Manufacturing	9000	9
Finance	3000	6
General Administrative	1500	5
Marketing	7500	$12\frac{1}{4}$

Keep Figures Simple

Keep your figures as simple as possible. Avoid algebraic symbols and other mathematical formulas unless you are doing a highly technical report in which they are absolutely essential. And round off figures when you can do so without misleading your reader. Accountants usually round off dollar amounts to the nearest $50 or $100 in general financial statements, omitting cents entirely. It is much easier to read $50 than $48.87, and $200 than $201.42—and the few dollar-and-cent differences are not important in a general interpretation of the amounts.

The same is true of percentages. It is sufficient to say in your narrative, "This represents a gain of nearly 12 percent," rather than, "This represents a gain of 11.872 percent."

Rounding off numbers is not always feasible, however. It may be very important to show exact figures. For example, the cost of manufacturing an automotive part may be $.0875, and if 500,000 are made, the total manufacturing cost is $43,750. If the unit cost were rounded off to $.088, the total manufacturing cost would be $44,000—a difference of $250. Exact figures are also important in price quotations, hourly pay rates, and so on.

When using figures in tables and graphs, try to keep the display simple by eliminating dollar signs and other value or quantity designations. Let your headings do the job for you. For example:

Office Furniture Inventory
Receptionist's Area

Item	Year Purchased	Estimated Life (years)	Depreciation Rate (%)	Present Value ($)
Desk	1972	15	15	80
Sofa	1978	5	20	400
Coffee table	1975	10	10	75
Typewriter	1977	5	20	100
Receptionist's chair	1978	8	20	175
Guest chair 1	Unknown	2	10	20
Guest chair 2	1976	5	20	135
Guest chair 3	1976	5	20	135

Note that by including quantity designations in the headings, we avoid the necessity of repeating years, %, and $ with each item.

Observe that in the table above we have omitted the "down rules." Some report writers like to box their tables completely (see the table on page 117) and to show down rules to separate the columns. This is a matter of preference. If the table is somewhat complicated and the numbers tend to run together, then by all means separate the columns with down rules. For most simple tables, however, the arrangement shown on page 115 is entirely satisfactory.

As mentioned earlier, when your report contains several tables (or even two on the same page), it is wise to number them. This is especially important when you want to make reference to a table in your narrative. The most common designations are, table, chart, and figure. The number becomes a part of the title of the illustration; for example:

Table 7. Earnings in Fourth Quarter

The table number and title are placed at the top of the table. The number and title of a chart or a figure may go above or below the illustration.

Interpret Your Figures

When figures are presented in tables or charts, you may have to interpret the most significant ones for your reader. For example:

The four most popular wage-payment plans used by the 1000 firms reporting are shown in Table 3 below.

Table 3.   Wage Plans Used in
1000 Companies

Plan	Number of Firms	Percent
Straight-time	690	69
Group or gang piece rate	150	15
Guaranteed piece rate	120	12
Group-bonus	40	4

It will be seen that the straight-time plan is still the overwhelming favorite—over 4½ times as popular as the second-ranked plan and twice as popular as the other three combined.

Use Graphs to Show Comparisons and Relationships

Business data is often presented on special graphs to help readers make comparisons and understand relationships. The three most commonly used graphs are the line graph, the bar graph, and the circle graph.

The Line Graph.   A table showing the ten-year sales growth of Dyna-Motion Corporation is shown below.

Dyna-Motion Corporation Sales Growth, 1972-1981			
Year	Sales ($)	Year	Sales ($)
1972	100,000	1977	400,000
1973	200,000	1978	500,000
1974	250,000	1979	500,000
1975	300,000	1980	700,000
1976	250,000	1981	1,000,000

The same information is presented on the line graph below. A line graph is most effective when it is used to show patterns, trends, and changes. You can see how much easier it is for the reader to see the pattern of sales growth (the "up" lines) and sales decline ("down" lines).

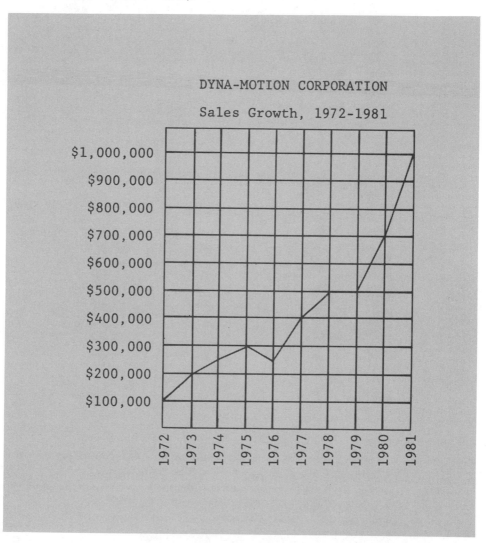

The line graph illustrated was prepared on graph paper, which can be purchased in various rulings in stationery stores. Because the lines on graph paper are sometimes hard to reproduce on the photocopier, you may have to do your own rulings. In this case it is customary to provide only marginal guides, as follows:

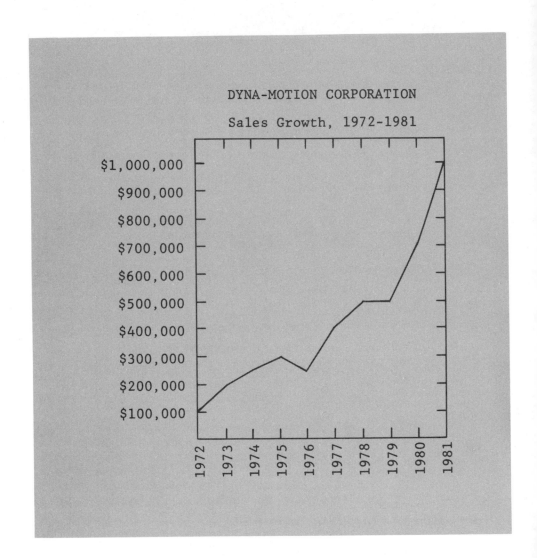

Line graphs are excellent visual devices for comparing one set of figures with another set. For example, Kirby Office Equipment Company compares the sales of typewriters with the sales of calculators for a ten-year period in the following line graph. Note that typewriters are indicated by a broken line and calculators by a solid line. This key is shown at the bottom of the graph.

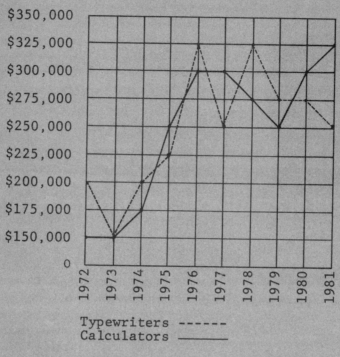

KIRBY OFFICE EQUIPMENT COMPANY

Sales of Typewriters and Calculators

1972 through 1981

Typewriters ------
Calculators ———

The Bar Graph. The bar graph is especially effective for displaying comparative data for a given time period. In the bar graph below, the manufacturing director of Tetron Incorporated shows the units produced by the firm's seven factories in 1982.

Barnsdall	37,000
Hopewell	39,000
Maywood	24,800
Kearney	28,000
Orino	34,000
Cobina	31,000
Laverne	39,500

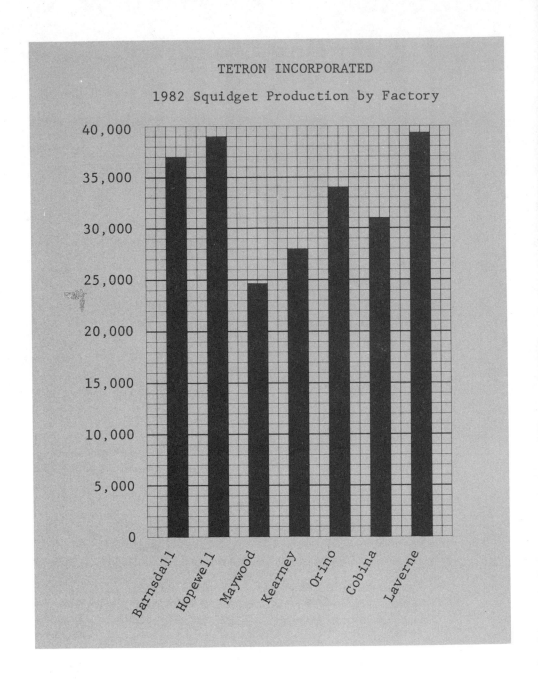

As you know, the bars on a bar graph may be either vertical (as above) or horizontal.

Another type of bar chart is the segment bar chart, in which each bar is divided into two or more segments. Each segment is given a different "texture" for contrast.

The following segment bar chart shows the quarterly earnings of Massey-Wilkes Oil Company for a nine-year period.

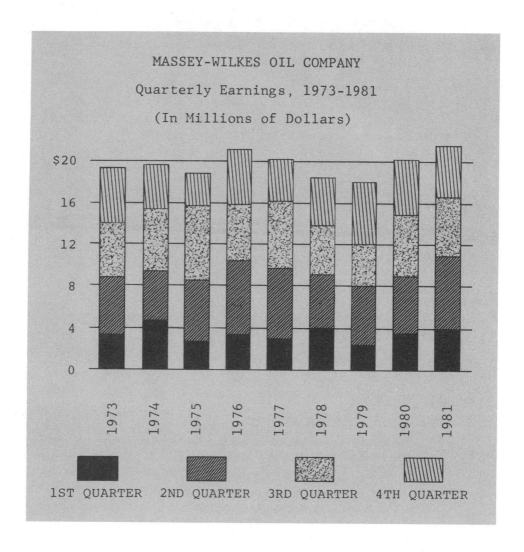

The Circle Graph. Circle graphs, or pie charts, are useful in showing the relationship of the parts of something to the whole. In the circle graph below, the advertising manager of Gladstone Products Company shows how the advertising dollar was spent in 1981.

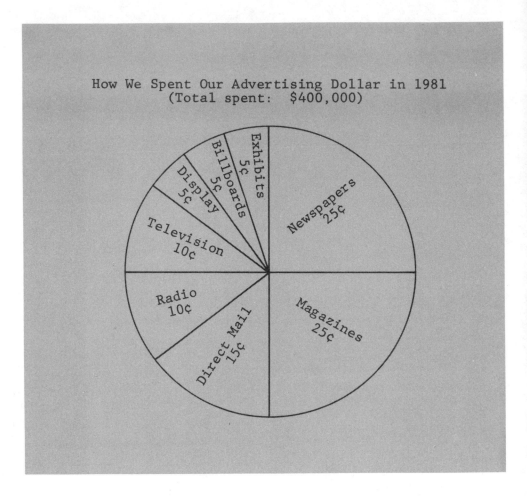

How We Spent Our Advertising Dollar in 1981
(Total spent: $400,000)

Exhibits 5¢
Billboards 5¢
Display 5¢
Television 10¢
Newspapers 25¢
Radio 10¢
Direct Mail 15¢
Magazines 25¢

Special Illustrations

We have shown you the simplest types of graphs that are used in business reports. These will serve your needs in most of the reports you will write; indeed, the occasions when you will want to use even these simple devices may be extremely rare. If display of numerical data *is* called for frequently, however, we suggest that you obtain one or more of the many books available on chartmaking. Graph preparation is an art, and the skill must be acquired through study and practice.

If you have the responsibility for preparing reports that are of a PR nature—such as annual reports to stockholders—it would be wise to engage the services of a professional designer. Often, special art work is called for—drawings, cartoons, photographs, "stick" figures, and so on.

HEADINGS

There are several ways to display your headings. Some writers prefer to center the first-level head and place all subordinate heads at the left margin, thus:

JOB EVALUATION   (first level)

OBJECTIVES OF JOB EVALUATION · (second level)

Adequate Job Data   (third level)

Hiring New Employees. It is especially important to . . .   (fourth level)

Others prefer the following sequence:

JOB EVALUATION

This is the first-level head, all caps and flush left, freestanding.

Objectives of Job Evaluation

This is the second-level head, upper and lower case, flush left, underlined, and freestanding.

Adequate Job Data.   The third-level head is also flush left, upper and lower case, underlined, and "run in"—that is, narrative copy starts on the same line.

Hiring New Employees.   The fourth-level head is indented five spaces, upper and lower case, underlined, and run in.

For very long, detailed reports, some writers use the traditional formal plan in setting up headings.

I. OBTAINING JOB INFORMATION

   A. QUESTIONNAIRE
      1. Essay Questionnaire
         a. Designing the essay questionnaire form
         b. Recording the information
      2. Checklist Questionnaire
         a. Advantages of the checklist questionnaire
         b. Designing the form
   B. OBSERVATION AND INTERVIEW COMBINATION
      1. Observation
      2. Interview
         a. Advantages
         b. Procedure
            (1) Setting for the interview
            (2) Participation of the applicant
               (a) Statement of clear objective
               (b) Departmental preferences

II. THE JOB DESCRIPTION

And so on.

We recommend that you use a simpler structure, such as one of those shown on page 123. Rarely, if ever, will you need to identify headings with roman numerals, letters, and numbers. Indeed, it is doubtful that in ordinary reports you will need more than four levels of headings. If you do, reexamine your report structure; you may be guilty of "overorganization."

Special Display of Headings

Some writers like to emphasize main headings by capping them and underlining them as well. Thus:

CHANNELS OF DISTRIBUTION

This is a matter of individual preference. However, we think that caps alone give sufficient emphasis and that by underlining all-cap headings the writer takes away some of the impact of those upper- and lower-case (ulc) headings that *depend* on underlining for emphasis. That is:

Direct Distribution

When you have relatively *short* main heads that are to be centered (chapter or section titles, for example), you can achieve good display by letter spacing; thus:

INVENTORY VALUATION

When you letter-space headings, however, you should underline them to pull the words together. Use three typewriter spaces between words.

ENUMERATIONS

By using enumerations (1, 2, 3, etc.), you can make your reports much easier to read and refer to. You saw many examples of enumerations in the reports you examined earlier in this book. They are especially effective in listing the steps in a procedure, presenting conclusions and recommendations, making summaries, and many other situations. Some writers introduce major topics by numbering them and then proceed to discuss them. Here is an example.

ELEMENTS OF A SYSTEMS STUDY

An effective systems study embraces four major elements:

1. Work distribution
2. Paperwork
3. Equipment
4. Layout

Work Distribution

Work distribution refers to the distribution of time, effort, skills, tasks, and work load. It . . .

Paperwork

Since the use of forms is often at the heart of a faulty system, ways must be found to eliminate, combine, simplify . . .

Equipment

Equipment includes any labor-saving device such as . . .

Layout

The layout of the office or other work station is . . .

The subheadings shown may also be numbered to help readers keep their place.

3. Equipment
   Equipment includes any labor-saving device such as . . .

BULLETS

You can also use "bullets" to make major points stand out. In a typewritten report, simply type a zero or lowercase o and fill it in with a felt-tip pen. Thus:

We found several advantages in centralizing the contract files:

- Elimination of duplication
- Safety of the records
- Saving of time
- Economy in equipment and space

On the other hand, there are good reasons not to . . .

INDENTATIONS

You can also achieve emphasis by special indentation of important material. Long quotations should always be indented. Following is an example.

THE BUDGET COMMITTEE

There appears to be a definite trend in larger companies to establish a budget committee. This committee is usually made up of the chief budget officer, the controller, and representative department heads and has the responsibility of setting general budget policies and seeing that realistic budgeting is carried out.

Having the line department heads participate is extremely important, according to Morris A. Sargent, in the September 1981 issue of Accounting Management. He says:

It is essential that department heads take an active part in the development of the budget and in putting budgetary controls into effect. The main reason is that this usually results in enthusiastic support of company efforts to operate within budget.

Assuming that a budget committee is a step in the right direction for Lone Star Distributors, it should probably be made up of the . . .

SUMMARIES

As mentioned earlier, in longer reports you may wish to prepare a summary at the end of each major topic. This not only gives emphasis to your discussion, but makes it easy for busy readers to concentrate on the highlights rather than read every word of the report. For example, assume that your report compares several communities as possible locations for a new retail outlet. Under the major heading SCOTTS HILL, you have discussed the factors that make this a favorable location as well as those that aren't so favorable. At the end of the discussion, you might summarize your points as follows. Notice that enumerations are used.

Summary

The pros and cons of a Scotts Hill location, then, can be summarized as follows:

Pros

1. A healthy economy and good growth possibilities
2. Limited competition
3. A good supply of skilled labor
4. An excellent environment

Cons

1. Remoteness from communication and transportation centers
2. Complicated political structure

YOUR TURN

Rewrite the following Recommendations section of a business report so that it is more readable, using whatever methods of display you prefer. Check your work against the solution on pages 199-200.

Given the foregoing weaknesses in our community relations, I recommend that we first develop a mailing list of civic-thought leaders and all identifiable members of the local power structure. This list would be used to distribute information concerning the company's position on such matters as labor disputes, price increases, expansion plans, pollution standards, corporate giving, and the like. Next, we should build and maintain good relations with the local press, radio, and TV. It is important that these people get, to the maximum degree possible, what they want and when they want it. Local editors and broadcast station managers should be supplied with the home telephone numbers of designated executives who can speak officially for the company. A third recommendation is that we do more in the way of institutional newspaper and radio-TV advertising, such as support of important community projects (the Bordentown Symphony, for example). Next, we should set up a speakers' bureau, providing speakers from the company, without charge, to local groups—schools and colleges, civic organizations, youth and senior citizens groups, etc. And finally, the company should be fully represented in such organizations as the Chamber of Commerce, Lions, Kiwanis, Rotary, and similar groups; and such professional organizations as the Society for the Advancement of Management, American Society of Chemical Engineers, American Marketing Association, Advertising Club, and Business and Professional Women.

A RESEARCH REPORT

Now let's look at another formally structured report. Following is the situation that brought about the report.

Consolidated Business Equipment Inc. employs 4500 people, 2000 of whom are located in the home office in Cincinnati and 2500 in twelve regional offices throughout the country.

As the company grows and new regional offices are opened, it becomes more and more difficult to maintain an effective communication link with the employees. At present, little is done to keep rank-and-file employees informed about major corporate decisions, new policies and procedures, and company progress and growth. Moreover, there is virtually no exchange of news and information among the various regional offices. Employees are often heard to complain that they "don't know what's going on."

The Administrative Committee has discussed the communication problem on several occasions and has decided that a study should be undertaken of the feasibility of establishing an employee newspaper or magazine as a medium of intracompany communications. The director of public relations, Alicia Saks, has been asked by the committee to make a study and present her conclusions and recommendations.

Preliminaries

In undertaking a study of this magnitude and complexity, the writer will have to spend a good deal of time thinking about how she will gather the required data and organize it so that readers can quickly grasp the message and arrive at a decision. When she is absolutely certain that she knows what the Administrative Committee needs in the way of information, she will prepare a working outline. As a safeguard against producing an irrelevant document, she will probably get reactions to this outline from the head of the committee and one or two other members before starting to draft the report.

Although definitely needed, the working outline is only a rough guide. It may change from day to day as material is gathered. This is almost a rule rather than an exception. Indeed, some writers don't attempt a final outline until they have made a rough draft of the entire report. Of what use is a final outline after a report is written? It tells the writer whether the sequence of coverage is right, whether main and subordinate headings fit, and whether the general setup is appropriate.

This report is to be read by several people, presumably the top executives in the corporation, and probably discussed in committee meetings. For this reason, Ms. Saks will choose an impersonal writing style.

In longer reports of this nature, the writer will also make certain that she:

1. Cites the authority for the preparation of the report (the Administrative Committee) and clearly describes its purpose
2. Defines terms that may cause confusion
3. States the perimeters of the study, indicating what the report does not cover as well as what it does
4. Includes the procedure used in gathering the information
5. Gives her specific conclusions and recommendations, as requested
6. Breaks up the copy with major and subordinate headings
7. Uses graphic illustrations where appropriate

The report prepared by Alicia Saks follows. As you read it, remember that the sequence of coverage, headings, and general setup represent only one person's idea. Another individual is likely to produce a report that is quite different from the one illustrated and yet equally effective.

But all good writers will have one common objective: to produce a report that is highly readable and easy to understand. More often than not, this means rewriting the report—perhaps two or three times—to achieve clarity, believability, and emphasis.

As you read the report that follows, pay attention not only to structure, language, and writing style but to the various methods used to achieve emphasis.

The following memorandum is written to transmit the report to the chairman of the Administrative Committee.

Consolidated Business Equipment Inc.
Interoffice Memorandum

To: Mr. G. L. Nagaki, Chairman
Administrative Committee

From: Alicia H. Saks

Subject: Company Newspaper Study

Date: November 17, 19--

Here is my study of the feasibility of establishing a newspaper
for employees of Consolidated Business Equipment Inc., which
you and the other members of the Administrative Committee
requested.

I have made a copy and bound it for each person on the committee. Do you want to distribute them or shall I?

                    A COMPANY NEWSPAPER
                          FOR
              CONSOLIDATED BUSINESS EQUIPMENT INC.

             A Report to the Administrative Committee

                            by
                      Alicia H. Saks
                 Director of Public Relations

                     November 17, 19--

Although a title page is not absolutely essential, it gives the report an air of importance. It is also a good place to show the authority for the report (the Administrative Committee), the author's name and title, and the date.

A COMPANY NEWSPAPER
FOR
CONSOLIDATED BUSINESS EQUIPMENT INC.

INTRODUCTION

The Administrative Committee of Consolidated Business Equipment Inc. has expressed concern about the increasing communications gap between management and employees, which is largely
the result of rapid company and branch office expansion.

When the company was small, it was relatively easy to keep
employees up to date on company activities through frequent
companywide meetings and occasional bulletins and announcements.
But today, with a staff of over 4500--and growing every year--
communication lines have been lengthened. Thus it has become
increasingly hard to keep employees informed about major decisions, new policies and procedures, and company progress and
growth. Equally important, there is no effective way to get
feedback from employees and bring them into the "management
circle."

One way to close the gap, the committee suggested, is to
issue an employee publication, and the writer was directed by
the chairman, Toshiro Nagaki, to undertake a brief study of the
matter and present her findings and recommendations. The results
of that study are detailed in this report.

Definitions

Various terms are used for employee publications, the most
common being house organ, newspaper, and magazine. These titles
are usually interchangeable, although in the publishing field
house organ has a special PR connotation. That is, such a publication is designed as much for outside image-building as for
internal communication.

The title of the report is repeated on the first page.

In the introduction the writer supplies the background, which includes need and purpose. If this were an informal memorandum report addressed to her boss, the writer would not have had to give this prefatory statement. But because the report is intended for several top executives—who may share it with others—this material is vital.

The paragraph indicates the authority for the report—that its preparation was not merely a whim but the result of a direct request.

Terms are defined in order to eliminate confusion.

2

There is little distinction between <u>newspaper</u> and <u>magazine</u>, even though each suggests a different size and format. In this report, the term <u>newspaper</u> is used. However, it should be remembered that this name has nothing to do with size, number of pages, binding, design, and so on.

<u>Scope</u>

In this brief study the author has not attempted to deal with all the factors that might be considered in deciding whether or not to publish an employee newspaper--for example, weighing cost of publication against the dollar value of the results. It is assumed that the Administrative Committee has determined the need for some type of publication, and this paper is simply a reinforcement of that need, with emphasis on the experience of other companies.

PROCEDURE

The writer used the following procedure to gather information for this report:

● Read a number of books and articles dealing with employee communications in general and with employee newspapers in particular. (A bibliography is available for any committe member who is interested.)

● Examined employee publications of 15 different companies in various parts of the country. Types of businesses represented include business equipment (King Inc., Blair-Jackson, American Seating, and Western Products), automotive supply, banking, publishing, retailing, and electronics manufacturing. (Samples of these publications are available for the committee's examination.)

● Talked with three chief editors of successful employee newspapers--one in Cincinnati, one in Detroit, and one in Providence--and corresponded with four others.

Here the author indicates the perimeters of the study, saying what the report does and does not cover. Such a statement is not necessary in every formally structured report, but it is appropriate here.

The heading PROCEDURE might have been a subordinate heading (like **Definitions** and **Scope**) under INTRODUCTION. This is a matter of choice.

A "bullet" is used to display each procedure. The author might also have enumerated these procedures (1, 2, 3, etc.), but enumerations are used frequently later in the report.

3

• Visited two printing firms in the Cincinnati area (Broadwell's and King Lithographers) and discussed production procedures, format, and cost.

• Talked with 23 Consolidated employees--agents, correspondents, secretaries, department managers, factory workers, and clerical people--in the home office as well as in the six branch offices.

PURPOSES OF AN EMPLOYEE NEWSPAPER

Authorities are in general agreement on the basic purposes of an employee newspaper. Vernon M. Lennon mentions five:*

1. To acquaint employees with conditions of employment; to show the company as a good place to work.

2. To create a family feeling among employees; to help them become familiar with their place in the organization; to show them the advantages of long company service.

3. To promote the reduction of accidents and waste and to increase productivity.

4. To answer employees' questions and to provide advance information about plans and policies.

5. To make plain to employees, their families, and the community that the company is a good corporate citizen and an asset to the area.

POPULARITY OF COMPANY NEWSPAPERS

A 1981 study of 1000 companies made by the Bureau of Business Research, University of Texas, revealed the following data concerning employee newspapers.

---

*Vernon M. Lennon, _Communication in Transition_, rev. ed., McGraw-Hill Book Company, New York, 1980, p. 468.

References to quoted sources are identified with an asterisk (*). If there are many such references, they are numbered (According to Lazarus Frey[2] . . .).

Details of the source of the quotation are given in a footnote at the bottom of the page.

4

PREVALENCE OF EMPLOYEE NEWSPAPERS

Number of Employees	Percent Having Employee Newspapers
Fewer than 1000	46.7
1000 - 4999	83.5
Over 5000	91.3

Source: Bureau of Business Research
University of Texas

As will be seen from the table, of the companies studied, 83.5 percent in the size category of Consolidated publish an employee newspaper. Incidentally, in a similar study made ten years ago, the figure was 77.2 percent, which would seem to indicate a growth trend in this communication medium.

Another study made last year (by Personnel Research Associates, Baltimore) indicates that there are now over 7000 employee publications in the country. These are circulated among 175 million readers at an annual cost of over $350,000,000.*

It would seem, therefore, that larger companies regard employee newspapers as effective--effective in the sense that the publication contributes to general morale, teamwork, and individual performance.

FREQUENCY OF PUBLICATION

The University of Texas study also revealed the following information about frequency of publication:

Monthly	81.5%
Biweekly	15.2%
Weekly	3.7%
Other	1.6%

*Rita C. Perrin, "Communicating with Employees," Personnel Digest, 14:76, October 17, 1979.

The author chose not to box or rule the table. Rules are helpful in tables that contain considerable data that might be confusing without them. In this case, they are not needed.

Immediately following the table is an interpretation of significant data.

Headings not only guide the reader but make the report visually appealing.

The footnote on the previous page is for a book. This one is for a magazine. Note that the style is slightly different.

5

SIZE OF PUBLICATION

The size of employee newspapers--in terms of overall dimensions and number of pages--varies a good deal. Of the publications examined, nine are 8½ by 11 inches and average eight pages in length. Editors who volunteered their recommendations, however, indicated that they were going to (or are considering going to) a "tabloid size" paper, such as 11½ by 15 inches.

CONTENT AND OTHER CONSIDERATIONS

Editors and others are strong in their belief that the newspaper should be for _employees_--not simply a vehicle for issuing management directives and propaganda. Although reports of company operations--sales and profits, expansion, new products, etc.--should be covered, most of the space, according to publishers, should be devoted to:

    o Promotions and other achievements of employees
    o Personal items (marriages, retirements, births, etc.)
    o Sports and other company recreational activities
    o An employee opinion exchange--e.g., letters to the editor
    o Photographs of employees at work, at play, and in social settings

As to the determination of actual content, experts recommend that a thorough study be made of the composition of the people who will read the paper--sex, ethnic heritage, education, and so on. This study will, they say, reveal valuable information as to emphasis, language level, and general content.

Editors, publishers, and other professionals emphasized over and over the importance of design--masthead, typography, layout, and overall graphics--to readership. They unanimously agree that the graphics should not be left to an amateur (such as an advertising artist or a local printer). Ms. Lisa McNeill, editor of an employee newspaper in Georgia, wrote:

6

   Employees invariably compare their company newspaper with commercial magazines they read, and they
expect the newspaper to be better! They insist on
a modern, sophisticated appearance--you might even
say "far out." Although we can't do everything they
want (four-color printing, for example), we did spend
a lot of money on professional design. And shortly
after we face-lifted <u>Grits</u> [the name of the news-
paper], giving it a completely new "tone," readership jumped dramatically.

   Especially important, too, is writing style. A publication
that reads like a management directive will, according to experts,
quickly destroy any hope of reaching the general employee. One
chief editor put it this way: "We learned the hard way that
an employee newspaper cannot be the voice of management and have
any real impact on employees. The language must be personal,
simple, conversational. Not a scandal sheet, to be sure, but
not a government report either."

COLOR

   Except for publications that are intended for public distribution (for example, du Pont's <u>Better Living</u>, Westinghouse's
<u>WE</u>, and Kaiser's <u>Westward</u>), company newspapers are generally
printed in one color. The main reason, of course, is cost.
Still, with the right graphics (and paper) a very handsome
one-color publication can be achieved.

STAFF

   Authorities are in total agreement that a really effective
employee newspaper cannot be produced without a full-time professional staff--reporters, editors, photographers, and production specialists. Most companies have a minimum of three

**Narrative quotations are
indented for emphasis.**

**A writer's insertion within a
quotation is bracketed.**

**Short quotations need not be
indented.**

7

full-time people: a chief editor, a reporter/photographer, and
a production editor. Some larger papers have six: an editor
in chief, two reporters, one photographer, and two production
editors.

COST

Assuming that Consolidated starts off with a full-time staff
of three, the per-copy cost, including production/printing, office
space and general overhead, and mailing and distribution, would
be about $1.25. If we print in quantities of 5000 and issue
an 8-page paper monthly, the annual cost would be in the neigh-
borhood of $75,000. This is a fairly rough figure, but it won't
be too far off.

CONCLUSIONS

Based on the information obtained from library research,
from interviews with editors and executives in various companies,
and from conversations with Consolidated executives and employees, there appears to be good justification for an employee
newspaper. Those who have had experience with these publications unanimously agree that a newspaper provides:

-- A first-rate medium for management in communicating
   with employees.
-- An effective device for obtaining feedback from employees
   on company policies and operations.
-- A good vehicle for establishing an atmosphere of
   "togetherness and belonging" on the part of employees.
-- An important method of developing good internal and
   external public relations.

According to research, the management in those companies
where employee newspapers have been published for several years
is satisfied that publishing costs are more than compensated
for by improved employee morale and productivity.

Here again, cost is an essential topic. It is not unlikely that some executives on the Administrative Committee will turn to this section first!

Any number of simple typewriter symbols can be used for display such as the one shown at the left.

8

RECOMMENDATIONS

It is recommended that:

1. Consolidated Business Equipment Inc. take immediate steps to establish a newspaper for employees.

2. The publication be issued once a month.

3. The size and format of the newspaper be in general tabloid dimensions, but the final decision to be made by the newspaper staff in consultation with local printers.

4. An editor in chief be employed at once and given authority to hire at least two additional staff members.

5. The responsibility for publishing the newspaper be given to the Public Relations Division. Even though the paper is not technically a PR medium, the employees in this division are accustomed to dealing with news and understand print media.

6. A Publications Advisory Committee be appointed to assist the editor in chief in determining content, format, writing style, etc. This committee would be permanent and made up of a representative of each division in the company. The president, director of public relations, and personnel relations manager would be _ex officio_ members.

As mentioned earlier, recommendations are usually numbered. This makes them easy to refer to when the report is being discussed in a meeting or in written communications.

Your Turn

Set up the following for easier reading. Use whatever headings and other devices you wish. (Compare your rendition with that on page 200.)

Many different types of incentive plans have been devised over the years. First, I will mention six of the early ones that received considerable attention but were abandoned one by one. Then I will describe in some detail the plan that is most widely used today—the Standard-Hour Plan.

The Halsey Plan provided that the bonus paid for increased productivity would be divided between employee and employer on a set basis—usually 50-50. In other words, an employee who produced at the rate of 60 percent got 30 percent, and the company kept 30 percent. The Bedeaux Plan also provided for the bonus to be shared. In this case, however, the incentive worker usually got 75 percent, and the remaining 25 percent was divided among indirect workers and supervisors. The Haynes Plan provided for the bonus to be shared by the worker, supervisors, and the company. Generally, this was 50 percent to the workers, 10 percent to supervisors, and 40 percent to the company. The Rowan Plan was based on a formula which increased bonus amounts at a *decreasing* rate as productivity increased. The Emerson Plan was similar to the Rowan Plan, except that it was based on a formula which increased bonus amounts at an *increasing* rate as productivity increased. The Gantt Plan provided a sharp increase in employee earnings, approximately 30 percent when the standards were first met. Thereafter, the bonus earnings were at the rate of 1.3 percent for each 1 percent increase in production. Today's most widely used incentive plan is the Standard-Hour Plan. Because of its popularity, it merits a full description, along with a discussion of its outstanding features.

HIGHLIGHTS OF CHAPTER 9

1. Use figures sparingly in reports.

2. Separate figures from narrative when feasible.

   Checkup. Separate the figures in the following paragraph by recasting them in a table. (See the suggested solution on pages 200-201.)

Although the straight-line method of depreciation was used on all office furniture and equipment, the annual rate of depreciation varied from item to item. For example, the original value of the desk computer was $3100, and the annual depreciation was $248. The annual rate of depreciation, then, was 8 percent. The filing equipment, which was purchased for $2720, was depreciated annually at $272, so the annual rate was 10 percent. The secretarial desk, which cost $325, was depreciated at $75 annually, a rate of 15 percent.

3. Keep figures simple.

   Checkup. (See the suggested solutions on page 201.)

   a. Round off the following to the nearest $100 for a financial report:

   $76,640.00
   $43,531.60
   $61,407.11
   $53,777.70
   $49,297.83
   $66,151.50

   b. Rewrite the following, simplifying the figures.

   In a recent poll, 62.76 percent of the employees indicated a preference for the earlier start-ing hour, but only 27.31 percent favored a thirty-minute lunch. Of the 615 employees who drive to work, 307 indicated difficulty in finding parking space, which amounts to 49.918 percent.

4. Interpret significant figures that appear in tables.

   Checkup. Supply a brief interpretation of the significant figures in the following table. (See the suggested solution on page 201.)

   The status of our accounts receivable as of September 30 is shown in the table below.

   | | Past Due | | | |
Not Yet Due	1-30 Days	31-60 Days	61-90 Days	Over 90 Days
34,200	25,900	5600	2700	1400
50%	36%	8%	4%	2%

5. Use graphs to show comparisons and relationships.

   Checkup. Complete the following sentences. (See page 201 for the correct answers.)

   a. The _____ graph is most effective in showing the relationship of the parts of some-thing to the whole.

   b. The _____ graph is best for displaying comparative data for a given time period.

   c. The _____ graph is most effective in showing patterns, trends, and changes.

6. Show ranks of headings properly.

   Checkup. Identify the following levels of heads. (See page 201 for the correct answers.)

   a. Flush left, freestanding, ulc, underlined

   b. Flush left, all caps

   c. Indented, ulc, underlined, run in

   d. Flush left, ulc, underlined, run in

7. Use enumerations, bullets, and other devices for lists.

PART 4

Steps in writing a research report

Most of the reports you write can be outlined and put together with a reasonable amount of planning and legwork—usually a few hours' worth. Now and then, however, you're likely to be handed a subject to write about that has special significance to the organization you work for, but which you know very little about. Such an assignment is an even greater challenge when the person who gave it to you knows little (if any) more than you do. The report may take weeks or months to complete.

Usually, these reports require research, and they must be treated in a somewhat scholarly manner—if not in language, cetainly in method. Your challenge is to enlighten the unenlightened, including yourself. More often than not, your research will involve reading, interviewing people, sending out questionnaires, and so on.

Longer research reports usually call for a lot of soul-searching and considerable legwork before you are ready to put down the first word. Following are the steps that you might take in doing these reports.

1. Define your purpose. You must be absolutely certain at the outset what you want (or are expected) to accomplish in your report.

2. Size up your audience. If you don't have a clear notion about who will read your report, you could be way off your target.

3. Make a preliminary statement of purpose and outline, and check them with the person who is most interested in your report—usually your boss.

4. Revise your statement of purpose and outline if necessary.

5. Gather your data.

6. Reread everything you have collected; then sort it into "families."

7. Rethink your outline again and nail down a final plan for writing.

8. Write the report in rough draft.

9. Edit your first draft (and maybe your second or third).

10. Type the final draft.

In this section, we'll cover these steps, using a typical research-report-writing situation.

CHAPTER 10

Getting your bearings

When faced with the task of preparing a report, some people can't resist the temptation to start to write immediately upon being handed the assignment. This works fine if you already have all the data you need and unlimited time. Usually, however, you have neither—especially unlimited time. In the first place, your deadline for finishing the job has a way of sneaking up on you. And to complicate matters, as you struggle to meet the deadline, you're probably expected to be on top of your regular job, which may be more than a full-time assignment itself.

So before you begin to do serious writing on a report that requires extensive research, you should do a lot of thinking about the problem and how you might offer a solution that will satisfy the people who want the information. It's essential that you find "where you're at"—get your bearings—before you do anything else.

SITUATION

Stillman Associates, a management consulting firm, was established fifteen years ago and has grown rapidly. Beginning with a small staff of 40, the company now employs over 400 people. The firm offers consulting services to business organizations in the areas of sales and marketing, personnel administration, financial management, manufacturing, and public relations.

In advising clients, Stillman executives and their assistants do a great deal of research, much of it from printed sources such as books and perodicals, and they write many reports. Each department in the company has its own small reference library. When information is required on a given subject, each individual must do his or her own library research, often enlisting the help of secretaries and other administrative personnel.

The arrangement is not satisfactory. In the first place, the number of publications available in a given department is necessarily restricted, and researchers are forced to scrounge around the company and local university and public libraries for materials. Not only do they often wind up empty-handed, they have spent a lot of time in the process.

There has been a good deal of talk for many months about the need for a central library, but nothing has been done about it. At a recent meeting of the Senior Staff Committee, the idea was presented formally to the president, H. W. Stillman. Although he thinks the time may have come for a company library, he wants more information. "I think there's no doubt that the need for a central library exists," he said. "But before we go off half-cocked, let's get some information. I know practically nothing about how such libraries operate, what they cost, how much space they require, and so on." Then he turns to you and says: "How about making a study of what's involved and giving this committee a report on what you find?"

DEFINING YOUR PURPOSE

Certainly you're not an expert on company libraries. Indeed, you have only a vague notion as to what the "study" referred to will involve. Probably no one else knows more than you do, but even so you will want to sound out some of the committee members.

However, before you start setting up appointments, you will want to go off by yourself and try to read the minds of the people who want the study made. You recall the discussion at the last staff meeting. Everybody there, including the president, seemed convinced of the need for a company library. Therefore, it would seem that you are not expected to *sell* the idea. Instead, you decide that yours is essentially a fact-finding mission. You are to enlighten the unenlightened. It won't hurt to reinforce the need for a company library, but your basic assignment, you conclude, is to answer five questions: What? How much? How? Where? and When?

When you have thought through the assignment, see if you can write out a tentative statement of purpose. It may not be *the* purpose, but it will help you get a bead on your target.

Your Turn

See if you can write a rough statement of purpose; then compare it with the one on page 201.

SIZING UP YOUR AUDIENCE

There is no doubt in your mind who the principal readers of your report will be—Stillman, the president, and the other members of the Senior Staff Committee. Thus it should be easy to answer such questions as: How much do they know about the subject? (Very little, so they'll need some orientation.) How much orientation? (Certainly a review of the present situation would be in order.) How long a report? (Not a tome, certainly. The president said to "take a few weeks" and didn't mention any help. So maybe 15 to 20 pages would do it.) What should be the form and writing style? (Since this is to be basically a factual report that will be used as an instrument for committee study, the report should probably be somewhat impersonal and structured for easy reference.) Are there biases to be reckoned with? (Apparently not; everyone seems to be of one mind.)

And so on. You mentally picture every member of the Senior Staff Committe and try to anticipate what she or he might expect from you in your study.

MAKING A TENTATIVE OUTLINE

Once you have prepared a rough statement of purpose and assessed your audience, you are ready to make a tentative outline of your study. At this point, you know that this will be a shot in the dark, but it will help you get a foothold and give you something to show the people you need to talk to. The first outline might be as follows:

Working title: COMPANY LIBRARY REPORT

INTRODUCTION

(Authorization, purpose, etc.)

NEED FOR A COMPANY LIBRARY

A. The situation now at Stillman Associates
B. Limitations of present setup

TYPICAL REQUIREMENTS IN OPERATING A COMPANY LIBRARY

A. Size (space and number of references)
B. Staff
C. Services provided
D. Operating rules and procedures

COST

A. Start-up
B. Operating

CHECKING YOUR PRELIMINARY PLAN

At this point, you are ready to check your preliminary plan with some of those who authorized the report. Take along your rough outline and your statement of purpose. It is at these meetings that you will learn specifically what the people want to know. So you ask a lot of questions (your solo deliberations triggered a good many) and you make notes. If you don't find out at these sessions what's on everybody's mind, you're not likely to later. This, after all, is not the biggest issue of the day among top executives, and you don't want to have to go back again and again.

REVISING YOUR PLAN

Based on your discussion with members of the Senior Staff Committee, you make substantial changes in your statement of purpose and your outline. These might now appear as follows:

A COMPANY LIBRARY FOR STILLMAN ASSOCIATES
(new working title)

INTRODUCTION

Purpose: To obtain for the Senior Staff Committee of Stillman Associates information from all reasonably available sources on the need for a company library, its functions and services, start-up and operating costs, location and layout, operating procedures, staff requirements, and place in the organization.

NEED FOR A COMPANY LIBRARY

A. Data obtained from previous company studies, if any
B. Data obtained from employees
    1. Materials now available in the company
    2. Procedures for obtaining materials from outside sources
    3. Limitations of present setup
    4. Estimated requirements of each department

REQUIREMENTS AND PROCEDURES

A. Size
    1. Space requirements (layout?)
    2. Number of references
B. Staff
    Number and qualifications
C. Services offered
D. General operating rules and procedures

COST

A. Start-up costs
    1. Room alterations, shelving, fixtures, etc.

2. Equipment

3. Initial acquisitions of library materials

4. Other (?)

B. Operating costs

1. Salaries and benefits

2. Continuing acquisitions (books, periodicals, etc.)

3. Supplies

4. Other (?)

LOCATION

Investigate available space (first-floor storage room?)

WHO AND WHEN

A. Place of the library in the organization structure

B. Effective date

Note that the outline does not include conclusions and recommendations. When you asked about this Mr. Stillman said they weren't necessary.

SCHEDULING YOUR TIME

When you asked about a date for submitting your report, June 10 was suggested since the monthly meeting of the Senior Staff Committee is that day. (It is now March 9.) Your next step is to set up some sort of schedule for completing the report. The dates will change of course—you'll frequently be ahead of schedule as well as behind schedule—but you'll reduce the risk of having the deadline creep up on you. For example:

May 1	All data gathered
May 15	All data sorted and organized
May 25	First draft completed
June 1	Second and other drafts completed
June 7	Typing, photocopying, and binding completed

Check your schedule at least once a week. When you see that you're falling behind, you may have to get on the phone or write letters to remind people to get requested materials to you.

Your Turn

Assume that you are special assistant to T. G. Mariposa, the director of manufacturing at Crown Manufacturing Company, which produces aircraft engines. During the past several months there has been an unusually large number of accidents and injuries in the factory, and the executives are alarmed.

Safety at Crown Manufacturing Company has always been a hit-or-miss proposition, and the increasing number of accidents would seem to indicate a serious need to do something about setting up specific safety rules and enforcing them.

You have been asked by your boss to make a thorough study of the accidents and injuries in the factory during the past six months in an effort to determine cause, responsibility, extent of injuries, and cost to the company. At the same time, you are to analyze accident prevention and safety methods as practiced in other companies and as recommended by authorities in manuals and handbooks, magazine articles, and special reports. Then you will prepare a report of your findings and offer your conclusions and recommendations.

As you mull over your assignment, you find a safety handbook in which six basic elements of an effective safety program are discussed:

1. Top management must promote safety; without its participation there is little likelihood of a program's succeeding.

2. Safety rules must be established for all workers and strictly enforced.

3. Safety training programs must be organized and conducted on an ongoing basis.

4. Employees should be given an important role in setting up and administering the program.

5. The overall responsibility for safety should be assigned to one individual—a specialist in safety education—who will direct the program.

6. Effective methods must be established for measuring safety performance.

See if you can develop a tentative outline for your study and write a preliminary statement of purpose. Check your solution with that on pages 201-202.

HIGHLIGHTS OF CHAPTER 10

Included in the initial stage of writing a research report are the following:

1. Define your purpose.
2. Size up your audience.
3. Make a tentative outline.
4. Check your preliminary plan.
5. Revise your plan.
6. Schedule your time.

Gathering and organizing your data

GATHERING DATA

The new outline, although by no means final, shows you the general route to your destination. Now you are in a position to start gathering the information you need for your report. You list the primary sources.

1. Check with various people to see whether a previous study was made on a company library (company archives?).

2. Talk with research people, administrative assistants, and others about their special needs and problems.

3. Visit libraries in the community—school, public, technical, and business—to see how they operate.

4. Send questionnaires to companies in various parts of the country who have first-rate libraries (is there an association of company librarians you can communicate with?).

5. Write to at least one major supplier of library equipment (American Seating?); maybe you can get a suggested layout.

6. Write or talk to one of your competitors (McKinsey?).

Company Interviews

When you decide to gather data by talking to people in the company, make plans for conducting the interviews in such a way that they are most productive. Obviously, you must have very clearly in mind what you want to find out before you begin your discussions.

Using your revised outline, you jot down the topics you want to cover at the interviews, organizing and reorganizing them so that like things are grouped together. The topics may be set up in questionnaire form. For example:

1. How many people in your department make frequent use of library resources?
   _____

2. What do you estimate as the percent of time spent by your department on library research? _____%

3. What periodicals does your department subscribe to?

_____

_____

_____

4. How many books were purchased last year for your department's use?

_____

5. How much did your department spend during the past year for books, periodicals, and other materials? _____

And so on. When in your interviews you are seeking mostly facts as opposed to mostly opinions, you may wish to send a brief questionnaire in advance and ask that it be completed prior to the meeting. This will save you a lot of time, particularly if the interviewee has to search the files or talk to other people while you are waiting. When the questionnaire has been completed ahead of time you can use the interview to review the data and clear up any questions about it.

Be sure to make a specific appointment for the interview, allowing yourself whatever time you think you will need—a half hour, hour, etc. If you don't, you are likely to find that your discussion is constantly interrupted by visitors, telephone calls, and other distractions.

Whether or not you use a questionnaire-type list of topics, be prepared to make notes at the interview. Use a separate page for each major topic. This will help you later when you start to sort the information you obtained.

Outside Interviews

The procedure for obtaining information by means of interviews with people outside the company will vary somewhat from in-company situations. In the first place, you probably will not send questionnaires in advance, since this may be an imposition. Second, your interview guide for outsiders will be less structured; indeed, it may be a simple list like this:

Services

Staff

Costs

Equipment and space needs

Procedures

Special suggestions

As a guest of the interviewee, you don't want to appear to be a polltaker, with pencil poised to check the appropriate box. Some researchers merely ask questions and listen, keeping pen and notebook hidden. Most people won't mind your making notes, however, if you ask, "Do you mind if I jot some of these points down as we talk?" Obviously, if you don't make notes, you will have to sit down at your desk immediately after the interview and reconstruct what was said.

It is especially important that people outside the company who are being interviewed understand why you want the information you seek. (In the library study, it is a good idea to ask Mr. Stillman to write a memo to each senior executive, asking for complete cooperation of all employees in your investigation, saying why the study is being made and its importance.)

When asking for an appointment by telephone from an outside person, you might introduce yourself like this:

> Mrs. Cavallo, my name is _____ . Stillman Associates is considering establishing its own company library for the use of its employees. Before we start to make our final plans, however, we want to get as much information as we can from people who operate successful company libraries. We are especially interested in such things as the services you offer, the size of your staff, equipment and space needs, and the quantity of materials you have. Could I spend some time with you in the next few days to get the benefit of your experience? I'll need about an hour.

Gathering Information by Mail

A letter requesting information requires special attention. Generally speaking, the individual from whom you seek information has little if anything to gain from cooperating with you. You should therefore observe these three hints in writing to people for special help.

1. Be especially courteous and tactful.
2. Give specific reasons why you want the information.
3. Make it as easy as possible for the recipient to respond.

You may include your questions in the letter itself or on a separate questionnaire form. In the latter case, which we recommend, you might send the following.

> Mr. C. R. Stevens
> Midwest Petroleum Corporation
> 122 South 39 Street
> Omaha, Nebraska   68131
>
> Dear Mr. Stevens:
>
> The Midwest Petroleum Corporation's company library is well known for its excellence, and I should like to avail myself of your expertise. We are considering setting up a company library at Stillman Associates, but before we do so we want to get as much guidance as possible from people like you.
> Would you be willing to take time from your busy schedule to answer some questions? The enclosed questionnaire has been designed to save you time, and I would be most grateful if you would complete it for me. I have enclosed an envelope for mailing it.
> Thank you!
>
> Sincerely yours,

Note that you will enclose a reply envelope; it should be addressed to you and a postage stamp affixed. Not only is this a must from a courtesy standpoint, you are much more likely to get a completed questionnaire. Most people feel guilty about tossing a stamped envelope in the wastebasket!

Following is an example of a questionnaire form you might use.

COMPANY LIBRARY STUDY
Stillman Associates

For ___Midwest Petroleum Corporation___

1. About how many employees are there in your company? _____

2. Roughly what percent use the company library regularly? _____

3. Approximately how many of each of the following are in your library now?

   Books _____

   Technical and professional
   society publications _____

   Special reports _____

   Other (please list) _____

   _____

   _____

   Periodicals _____

   Catalogs _____

   Pamphlets _____

   _____

   _____

   _____

4. Please list by title the members of your library staff.

   _____

   _____

   _____

5. What, approximately, are the room dimensions of your library?

   _____ feet by _____ feet

6. Please check each service provided by your library staff.

   a. Review new publications and place orders for them _____

   b. Abstract important papers on request _____

   c. Clipping services _____

   d. Route periodicals to employees _____

e. Bibliographical research for employees   _____

f. Obtain materials through interlibrary loan   _____

g. Other (please list) _____

_____

_____

We have shown you only the first page of the questionnaire that might be sent for the library study. Rarely should your questionnaire exceed two pages. The reason is, of course, that people are busy. So if you're determined to keep yours to two pages, you may have to make choices. Just be sure that in those two pages you have covered the topics that are most important to you in your study.

It's a good idea to include your name and address at the bottom of the second page. Although you will supply an envelope with this information, it may become detached.

Here are specific hints for framing your questionnaire:

1. Allow plenty of space for answers.
2. When possible, line up your answer spaces (see items 3 and 6 in the questionnaire illustrated); this will make tabulation easier later.
3. Try to arrange your questions in the order of their importance to you.
4. Make certain that each question is clear. (Have someone in your office read the questionnaire before you mail it.)
5. In general, try to avoid "how" and "why" questions; they require too much time to answer. This type of information is best obtained at a personal interview.

Reading

Much of the information you obtain for your reports may come from reading—magazines, newspapers, pamphlets, special reports, and so on. If you need help in locating materials on the subject you are investigating, talk to a professional librarian.

General References. Although there may be few, if any, relevant publications on hand in the library you are visiting, there will undoubtedly be indexes to books and periodicals from which you can locate names of publications that you can obtain elsewhere. The best place to look for magazine articles, according to subject, is the *Reader's Guide to Periodical Literature;* for newspaper articles, *The New York Times Index;* and for books, *Books in Print.*

Making Notes. As you read, you will want to make notes. Cards are best for this purpose—3 by 5 inches, or 4 by 6 inches, or 6 by 9 inches. Cards are sturdy and can be sorted and re-sorted easily. Be sure to identify the sources of your material; you may wish to quote from the book or periodical, in which case you will want to give credit in your report to the author and publisher. Here are two rules to follow in making notes on cards:

1. Write on one side of the card only.

2. Limit each card to one subject.

Usually your notes will appear in the form of summary statements. Because there is little continuity when you read several different authors, each with a different approach to the subject, you will probably find it difficult to outline as you make notes.

Following is an example of notes you might make from your reading.

> Space
>
> Open shelves preferable. Must allow for growth -- a technical library may duplicate itself every 12-15 years. Periodicals may grow at rate of 7 in. of shelf space each year per title. Larger periodicals inc. at rate of 10 in./yr. Probably min. space required for 1,000 bound vols. is 20 x 35 ft.
>
> Brehn, "Your Company Library"
> Admin. Management,
> Sept. 1980, pp. 14-18

Note the use of the "slug" line at the top of the card—SPACE. This helps you to spot the subject of the notes quickly—very useful later when you sort your notes. Complete information about the source of the material is given at the bottom.

ORGANIZING THE DATA

When you have gathered all the information you need for your report, you are ready to begin a final plan. This is a critical step. Some writers start their final plan just as soon as the data starts to accumulate. Certainly, it is a good idea to set up some sort of recap procedure for the completed questionnaires as they arrive. This gives them a "leg up" on the sizable chore of sorting and classifying the mass of data. A final writing plan, however, is usually not attempted until everything is in.

In any event, while you were listening and reading, you undoubtedly made a lot of notes. Now you have the job of sorting and organizing the information. At this point you realize the wisdom of using a separate sheet or card for each major topic. If you had not done this, you would now either have to make elaborate cross-references or cut the notes apart.

When all the information is in, it's a good idea to read it all again before making a final writing plan. At this stage, you may decide that for some of the topics you intended to cover, your data is very skimpy. So you have to decide whether to "pad out" these gaps, go with what you have, or eliminate this material. In other cases, you may have amassed data that you now consider irrelevant. Only by a careful reading of your notes—preferably with one eye on your latest outline—can you get the whole perspective.

Once you've familiarized yourself with what you have in the way of data, you are ready to sort it. Sorting is something like arranging a hand that you have been dealt at bridge or other card games. You put your suits together and arrange the cards within each suit in some fashion, depending on the game.

For the sorting process, you will probably have six stacks of notes and other materials:

Introductory Material

Need

Requirements and Procedures

Cost

Location

Who and When

For each of these six stacks you will want to re-sort your notes according to the subheads in your outline. For example, under the main head REQUIREMENTS AND PROCEDURES you might have four separate batches:

Size (space requirements, number of references)

Staff (number and qualifications)

Services Offered

General Operating Rules and Procedures

Depending on the size of each of these batches, use a paper clip or rubber band to hold the materials together.

When all your notes have been sorted, lay out the stacks on a large table. Now you can see at a glance the general framework of your report. If your planned arrangement doesn't suit you, you can shift the "families" of topics about until you have exactly what you want. When you know you have nailed down the best plan for your report, you are ready to set down your final outline—the one from which you will write.

YOUR TURN

Assume that in preparing the safety report (page 148) you read the following on page 316 in the manual, *Safety in Industry,* by G. R. Conover, published by McGraw-Hill in 1980:

> Group or mass training has a place in a complete safety program, but it is far more effective to use a personalized or individual safety-training approach. The advantages of a personalized approach are many. Hazards vary on each job, and because of individual differences, might even vary for employees on the same job. These individual differences can be considered if the safety program is personalized. Personalized safety training permits consideration of the worker's rate of learning, interests, natural ability, and physical limitations. The training can be specific, whereas group training must be general. The key to successful job-safety training is telling the employee what the hazards are on his or her particular job and how to avoid them.

On a 6 by 9 card, make notes on the above passage; then compare the results with the suggested solution on page 202.

HIGHLIGHTS OF CHAPTER 11

In preparing to gather data for your report:

1. Try to find out whether a previous study has been made on the subject.
2. Make a list of people—in the company and outside—whom you want to talk with personally; once you have determined exactly what you want from these people, set up specific appointments.
3. If there are people outside the company from whom it is not feasible to obtain information in person, prepare a questionnaire so designed that the least possible time is required to complete it.
4. Make complete notes of relevant information obtained from your interviews.
5. Find out what pertinent information is available from printed sources; as you consult these sources, make notes on cards, identifying the source.

Writing the report

If your data is complete and is intelligently sorted, writing the report should not be difficult. You can start anywhere you want to, of course. Most writers, however, find it best to follow the sequence of the final outline.

In any event, it is important to put together a rough draft of the entire report as quickly as you can, keeping in mind as you write that you will rewrite. Remember that the need to rewrite is not a sign of incompetence. Indeed, the best, most experienced writers rewrite, not just once but two or more times. It is the once-over-lightly writer who generally produces badly organized, unreadable reports. If veteran writers expect to revise their original draft at least once, it stands to reason that the beginner is not likely to get by with one stab at the assignment.

As editor of your own material, you should learn some basic proofreaders' marks. Following are those you will find most useful.

Symbol	Meaning	Example
⌒	close up space	t͜heir decision was
∼	transpose	at the ⁀meeting⁀ April
¶	start a new paragraph	job.¶.The final outcome
≡	capitalize	of the e̲m̲ployee b̲e̲nefits c̲o̲mmittee
≣	all capital letters	Results in May
⸋	delete	to the May⟋Fair Corporation
⸤⸥	delete and close up space	take ~~extreme and~~ unusual precautions
· · ·	stet (leave as it was)	agree with the ~~Committee's~~ findings
/	lowercase	in the ⟋company's best interests
no ¶	no paragraph	no¶ So nothing was gained by
○	spell out	and ⑧were in favor of

HEADINGS

Before you start to write, study the structure of your outline and see how many levels of heads you will need. For this report, it would seem that four levels will be sufficient.

Assuming you will have no centered heads (except for the title of the report on the first page), let's review the heads you might choose for your report:

COST
This is your first-level head in the report. It is all caps and flush left, freestanding.

Size of Library
This is the second-level head, upper and lower case, flush left, underlined, and freestanding.

Space Requirements. The third-level head is also flush left, upper and lower case, underlined, and run in.

Tables and Chairs. The fourth-level head is indented five spaces from the left margin, upper and lower case, underlined, and run in.

GETTING STARTED

As mentioned, it is important that you get something down on paper as quickly as you can. Some writers make a thoroughly detailed outline of each major section before they start to write—much more detailed than the outline used in gathering and sorting the data. Others find it easier to simply begin writing, with the idea that the first draft serves only as a starting point for one or more revisions.

No matter how you prefer to go about it, we emphasize again the importance of editing your work. At the left on the following pages is a first draft you might write for the introduction to the company library report; at the right is the same copy edited.

First Draft

INTRODUCTION

Stillman Associates is essentially a research organization.
Obviously it serves its many clients by providing valuable advice
in all areas of management. However, more often than not the
advice given is based on research, often from printed sources.
Indeed, the printed word can be thought of as basic "raw material," just as iron ore is the raw material for a steel manufacturer.

Yet the company is woefully lacking in this raw material.
Each of its major revenue centers--sales and marketing, personnel
administration, financial management, and public relations--main-
tain their own library of printed materials none of which are
adequate. Hardly a subject being researched, according to
operating executives, can be researched within the confines of
our present resources. Nine times out of ten, the person doing
the research is forced to scrounge materials from other divisions,

INTRODUCTION

Stillman Associates is essentially a research organization.

~~Obviously~~ it's [*revenue is derived mainly from*] ~~serves its many clients by~~ providing ~~valuable~~ advice [*to clients*]

in all areas of management. However, more often than not, the

advice given is based on research, [*usually*] ~~often~~ from printed sources.

Indeed, [*to Stillman Associates,*] the printed word can be thought of as basic "raw mate-

rial," [*in the same way that*] ~~just as~~ iron ore is the raw material for a steel manufac-

turer.

Yet the company is woefully lacking in this raw material.

Each of its [*five*] major revenue centers--sales and marketing, personnel

administration, [*manufacturing,*] financial management, and public relations--main-

tain[*s*] ~~their~~ [*its*] own library of printed materials, none of which [*is*] ~~are~~

adequate. Hardly a subject ~~being researched~~ [*under investigation*] ~~according to~~

~~operating executives~~, can be researched within the confines of

our present resources. Nine times out of ten, the person doing

the research is forced to scrounge materials [*anywhere it can be found-within the company?*] ~~from other divisions~~,

2

outside libraries, and other sources. This lack of immediately

available resources presents two basic problems:

　　1. The time required to find appropriate materials, which

often results in delayed reports to clients.

　　2. Duplication--not only of staff effort but of in-house

resources

　　For these and other reasons, senior staff members have been

agitating for a central company library. This matter was brought

up at the March meeting of the Senior Staff Committee and

thoroughly reviewed. It was at this meeting that Mr. Stillman

suggested that a thorough study be made of need, space required,

cost, services, and operating procedures.

Purpose

　　The purpose of this report, then, is to obtain for the

Senior Staff Committee information from all reasonably available

sources on the need for a company library, its functions and

services, location and layout, operating procedures, staff

Editing of First Draft

from   from

   outside libraries, and other sources. This lack of immediately

                          main

available resources presents two ~~basic~~ problems:

                    locate

    1. The time required to ~~find~~ appropriate materials, which

                 services

often results in delayed ~~reports~~ to clients.

    2. Duplication--not only of staff effort but of in-house

resources⊙

    For these and other reasons, senior staff members have ~~been~~

recommended that the company establish a central

  ~~agitating for a central company library~~. This matter was brought

up at the March meeting of the Senior Staff Committee and

thoroughly reviewed. It was at this meeting that Mr. Stillman

requested   costs;

~~suggested~~ that a thorough study be made of need space required,

~~costs~~ services, and operating procedures.

Purpose

                              provide

    The purpose of this report, then, is to ~~obtain for~~ the

                  with

Senior Staff Committee information from all reasonably available

sources on the need for a company library, its functions and

services, location and layout, operating procedures, staff

3

requirements, and place in the organization. It also attempts

to answer the question, when?

Delimitation

In making this study and writing the report, the author did

not weigh the pro's and con's of a company library for Stillman

Associates. It was assumed that there were virtually no arguments

against a company library. Therefore, the author's emphasis is

on what, who, how, how much, and when rather than on why there

is should (or should not) be a company library.

Editing of First Draft

requirements, and place in the organization. It also attempts

to answer the question, when?

Emphasis

~~Delimitation~~

In making this study and writing the report, the author ~~did~~ [spent little time]

~~not~~ weigh[ing] the pro's and con's of a company library~~, for Stillman~~

~~Associates.~~ It was assumed that there were virtually no arguments

against ~~a company library~~ [the idea]. Therefore, the author's emphasis is

on what, who, how, how much, and when, rather than on why there

~~is~~ should (or should not) be a company library.

Does it strike you that the changes made in the editing of the first draft are over-done? If, as recommended, you simply "splash" something down with the purpose of revising it, your edited draft will look similar to the one illustrated—maybe worse. Indeed, it is not unusual for a writer to switch ideas around, eliminate entire paragraphs, and finally wind up with a big X over the entire draft—which simply means to start over again. It is at this point that she or he will make an outline before attempting a revision.

Not every change illustrated is mandatory, nor do we say that additional changes wouldn't improve the copy. Every writer will have a different idea how the copy should read. The important thing is to use the first draft to rethink your message. More often than not, you will find such shortcomings as:

- Deadwood—using more words than necessary to express your ideas
- Redundancies—using two words that mean the same thing; for example "First and foremost . . ."
- Using words that have negative connotations; for example, "executives have been agitating" instead of "executives have recommended that"

- Rambling, overlong sentences and paragraphs
- "Businessese" or "federal" terms; for example, "Pursuant to the president's directive, the writer undertook an investigatory study of the problem in an effort to bring clarification in terms of its significant implications"
- Poor transition between sentences and paragraphs; for example, lack of such connectives as *also, on the other hand, however, at the same time,* and *finally*

DISPLAYING DATA

Use every chance to display your data. Remember that white space in a report is always welcomed. We don't mean that every report should be loaded with headings and enumerations—having too many is just as bad as having too few. But most report writers err on the side of too few, so look for opportunities to use "bullets," enumerations, headings, etc., to break up solid copy. Page after page of solid type with no "visual breaks" is tough going, no matter how well written the material is.

Notice how enumerations lighten up the following copy.

LOCATION AND LAYOUT

Perhaps the best location for the library is the storage area on the first floor. (The supplies and equipment now housed there can be transferred to a nearby commercial warehouse.) This location is especially good for four reasons:

1. It is easy to get to by elevator and stairways.
2. There is plenty of room (40 by 40 feet).
3. It is safe in that it can easily handle a floor load of 150 pounds per square foot (recommended by the American Library Association).
4. It is well ventilated, quiet, and well lighted (60 foot-candle, shadowless illumination).

Use tables, drawings, graphs, etc., when they will help readers understand your discussion. Following are examples.

COST

Two types of costs must be considered: start-up and operating.

Start-Up Cost

Based on information received from company libraries, suppliers, and two local contractors, the following table shows the estimated start-up cost of the size of company library that would meet Mr. Stillman's initial needs.

Estimated Start-Up Cost

Alteration of storage room	$ 8,800
Equipment	14,000
Books (initial order)	7,500
Subscriptions (initial order)	4,500
Pamphlets and other materials	1,000
Miscellaneous supplies	1,800
Total	$37,600

As will be seen, the cost of equipment and the initial cost of printed materials are about the same ($14,000 and $14,800, respectively). Miscellaneous supplies include only stationery, folders, cards, and the like. No provision was made for the purchase of microfilm and microfiche supplies (nor are readers included in the equipment figure). Eventually, however, such supplies and equipment will be required.

Under the heading LOCATION AND LAYOUT, you will probably want to include a drawing such as this:

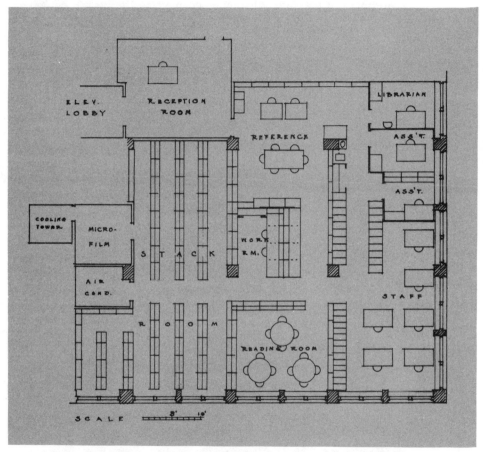

You will see that we have provided for three "carrels" (booths). These are invaluable for reading microfilm and microfiche, using computers for instruction, and listening to tapes and records. Etc.

About Illustrations

1. Give each table or drawing a title. Titles of tables go at the top; titles of drawings may be placed at the top of the illustration or at the bottom. If your report contains a great many tables or drawings to which you refer frequently in the body of the report, it is wise to give each a number, such as Table 1, Figure 7, etc.
2. Interpret each table or drawing immediately following the illustration.

ELEMENTS OF THE REPORT

Title Page

Since the company library report is to be distributed to members of the Senior Staff Committee for group discussion, it is best to structure it somewhat formally and place it in a binder. Thus there should be a title page.

The title page usually contains at least three elements: the title of the report, the author, and the data. Also included may be the person or persons for whom the report was written.

The title itself should be as brief as possible, yet convey immediately what the report contains. You decide on A COMPANY LIBRARY FOR STILLMAN ASSOCIATES, and your title page might appear as follows.

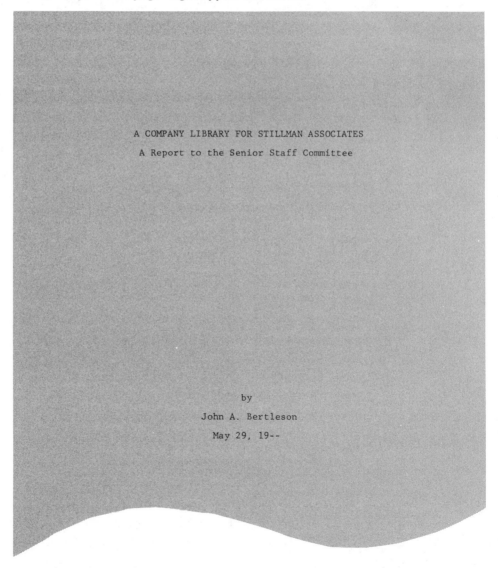

A COMPANY LIBRARY FOR STILLMAN ASSOCIATES

A Report to the Senior Staff Committee

by

John A. Bertleson

May 29, 19--

Table of Contents

You may decide to include a table of contents; however, in relatively short reports it isn't essential. The table of contents, which comes right after the title page, consists of the major headings and subheadings and page numbers. For example:

TABLE OF CONTENTS

And so on. Note the use of leaders (. . .). These help to guide the reader to the page number.

List of Illustrations

Some reports contain so many illustrations—tables, graphs, drawings, printouts, etc.—that a list of them is given following the table of contents or as a part of it. This list shows the title of the illustration, number (if any), and page number, thus:

Figure 12: Feedback Loop in a Central Heating System   27

Appendix

Here you place supplementary data the reader may be interested in, such as a copy of the questionnaire you used to gather information; additional tables, graphs, and drawings; and clippings from periodicals and reports.

Bibliography

If your report is based primarily on information obtained from books, periodicals, and other printed materials, and you have reference to these sources in your report body, it is wise to include a list of references (alphabetically by the last names of the authors) at the end of the report. This bibliography shows the author's name, the title of the publication, edition (if appropriate), publisher, and date of publication. Here are sample entries for different types of materials. A model bibliography is shown below.

BOOKS

Raiford, Sarah T., *Effective Employee Orientation,* McGraw-Hill Book Company, New York, 1980.

Simank, J. W., and R. J. Pederson, *Visual Aids in Employee Training,* Harcourt Brace Jovanovich, Inc., New York, 1981.

Theissen, Peter C. (ed.), *Personnel Handbook,* Prentice-Hall, Inc., Englewood Cliffs, N.J., 1977.

MAGAZINES

Millard, Theresa, "How Effective Are Employee Handbooks?" *Journal of Personnel Management,* Vol. 37, No. 1, pp. 1-9, October, 1980.

Salow, Christopher, "A New Approach to Employee Orientation," *Administrative Quarterly,* 20:32-47, 1979.

GOVERNMENT PUBLICATIONS

U.S. Department of Health and Human Resources, *The Employee's Right to Know,* 1980, U.S. Government Printing Office, Washington, D.C.

————— , *Survey of Current Business: 1980 Supplement,* U.S. Government Printing Office, Washington, D.C., 1981.

MISCELLANEOUS

Editorial, *Los Angeles Times,* October 11, 1980, p. 14, col. 1.

"The Business Classroom Boom," *Houston Chronicle,* March 13, 1978. p. 14, col. 2.

Mendoza, C.K., "Management Teamwork," unpublished paper delivered to the Syracuse Administrative Management Society, November 16, 1977.

THE TRANSMITTAL MEMORANDUM

You will need to write a brief memorandum transmitting the report to those who asked for it. Usually, this memorandum is paper-clipped to the outside of the binder, although some writers like to put it inside the binder. Following is the memorandum that might be written to transmit the company library report to the Senior Staff Committee.

Stillman Associates

Interoffice Memorandum

TO: Senior Staff Committee   FROM: John A. Bertleson

SUBJECT: A Company Library for Stillman   DATE: May 29, 19--
Associates

Here is my report on a company library for Stillman Associates. This study was requested by the committee at its March meeting.

If additional information would be helpful, I will of course be glad to supply it.

JAB

Distribution:

H. W. Stillman
Agatha Mimms
C. R. Roudabush
Paul D. Taussig
Katherine P. Uethe
H. L. Vincenzi

TYPING THE FINAL COPY

When you are ready to have the report typed, you will need to give the typist specific instructions on spacing, margins, and paging.

Spacing The Report

Although it is not wrong to single-space your report, we recommend that you use double spacing. You'll use more paper, of course, but because white space makes a report so much easier to read, the additional cost is worth the investment.

Paragraph Indentations

Indent each paragraph five spaces from the left margin.

Establishing Margins

Every report should have at least a one-inch margin on each side as well as at the top and bottom. If the report is to be bound, leave another one-half inch at the binding edge.

Numbering the Pages

Number all pages (except the "front matter"—title page, table of contents, etc.) in the upper right corner about one-half inch from the edge of the paper and flush with the right margin.

If you decide to add pages after the report has been typed and page-numbered, you can make insertions using a, b, c, etc. That is, if you want to insert a new page between pages 5 and 6, number it 5a. Then at the bottom of page 5 write "Page 5a follows." On the other hand, if you have left out a page number—for example, if there is no page 47—you can renumber page 46 as 46-47.

PROOFREADING THE REPORT

When the final draft of the report is typed, it must be proofread. This is best done by two people—one holding the clean copy and checking it as the other reads aloud from the draft from which the final copy was made. Take your time. Good proofreading is an art. Pay particular attention to punctuation (often ignored in proofreading) and capitalization. Double-check all figures; this is where some typists make most of their errors.

MAKING COPIES

With photocopying machines available in most offices, there isn't the need there once was to make carbons. However, you ought to make at least one carbon for insurance—in case the original disappears. Usually, however, the carbon does not need to be corrected.

YOUR TURN

Following is a first draft of a section of a marketing report. It needs editing. It is overwritten, there are several redundancies, and some of the statements are "muddy." Make a new draft that you think will be easier to read and understand; then compare it with the version on pages 202-203.

LEADERSHIP DUTIES AND RESPONSIBILITIES OF DISTRICT SALES MANAGERS

Authorities are in general concurrence on the six significant leadership duties and responsibilities of district supervisors. These are to:

1. Explain, discuss, and interpret the varied and myriad company policies that relate to employees and the general public.
2. Maintain a sufficient and adequate district sales force supported by an ample, well-trained administrative contingent which is properly motivated.
3. Maintain continuing and ongoing programs of salespeople development through scheduled on-the-job training consultations with supervisors and salespeople.
4. Initiate and conduct an annual performance review with supervisors and salespeople to develop the areas in which training assistance for each individual should be directed.
5. Ensure top-quality salesmanship starting with the personnel recruitment process and continuing indefinitely with proper training, supervision, and control.
6. Improve, to the extent viable and feasible, the company's image in terms of both employees and the public-at-large.

HIGHLIGHTS OF CHAPTER 12

In putting together the final report:

1. Use your final outline and the materials you have gathered to create a rough draft as quickly as you can, keeping in mind that you will rewrite it later.
2. Study the headings you have selected: Do you have sufficient number? Is each heading of the right level? Etc.

3. As you study your first draft, look for deadwood, redundancies, rambling sentences, "businessese" or "federalese" terms, poor transition, etc. Use proofreaders' marks to indicate changes.

4. Use every chance to display your data by the use of "white space," indentations, and illustrations.

5. As for illustrations:
   a. Give each table or drawing a title. Titles of tables go at the top, and titles of drawings may be placed at the top of the illustration or at the bottom.
   b. If you have a great many tables or drawings, give each a number.
   c. Interpret each table or drawing immediately following the illustration.

6. When you have made all the corrections, deletions, and additions needed and know that the final draft is the best you can do, give the typist complete instructions on spacing, paragraph indentations, margins, and pagination.

7. Prepare a title page and, if necessary, a table of contents, a list of illustrations, an appendix, and a bibliography.

8. Draft a letter of transmittal.

9. Proofread everything carefully, preferably with another person holding the draft or final typewritten copy.

10. Make the appropriate number of copies for distribution.

11. Bind the report.

Business letters as reports

Letters that go to people outside the company are also reports. The most obvious difference between a letter and an interoffice memo report is form. The reason for having a memorandum form is, of course, to save time and money. You don't need an elaborate inside address or even a salutation or a "Sincerely yours." And the quality of interoffice stationery need not impress anyone.

On the other hand, since letters to outsiders are often PR instruments, they deserve a good deal more window dressing. Attention is given not only to sophisticated letterhead design and high-quality paper, but to an inside address, salutation, complimentary closing, and other mechanical niceties.

It has been argued that such mechanics are Victorian and do not belong in twentieth-century communications. "Why," critics ask, "should you address a complete stranger as *Dear Mr. Doe* when Mr. Doe is not specially dear? Or sign off as *Sincerely yours* when *yours* implies possession?" These are perfectly logical questions, but traditions live on, and few correspondents are willing to break them for fear of offending the reader. As foolish as *dear* and *yours* seem, these expressions do add some warmth to communications, and for that reason alone they seem destined to be around a long time.

Because letters go to people of influence—or potential influence—writers are encouraged by management to be especially careful about courtesy, tact, promptness, and precision in language. Of course, courtesy, tact, promptness, and language precision apply to informal company reports too, but they are not as important as in letters. The situation brings to mind the parental edict we've all heard since we were two: "Mind your manners when company comes."

Business letters can be effective in increasing sales, getting better service from suppliers, and simply persuading the general public to think good things about you. Obviously, they can do just the opposite. Customers are not likely to have any special loyalty to companies whose letter writers are blunt and tactless. And those who might *become* customers or investors can be quickly dissuaded by pompous, overbearing, illiterate correspondents. So the dollar sign becomes an important guidepost in planning and writing letters.

CHAPTER 13

Writing effective letters

GUIDELINES FOR LETTER WRITING

Although there is no set formula that will guarantee you the right letter on every occasion, there are eight general guidelines that, if followed, will give you a better chance of producing effective letters:

1. Avoid formulas.
2. Make your letters human.
3. Deal with the subject at hand.
4. Stress the positive.
5. Use the right timing.
6. Say *no* gently.
7. Do a little more than you have to.
8. Confirm important agreements by letter.

Avoid Formulas

Many correspondents have been led to believe that letters can be written by formula. That is, just as a chemist or chef mixes certain ingredients in precise quantities to produce cough syrup or a soufflé, the writer applies the "rules of writing" to every letter and comes up with the perfect communication. The trouble with this notion is that there aren't hard-and-fast rules about letter writing. The reason is that the "ingredients" of a letter depend on who the reader is and what that reader is likely to respond to most favorably.

Satisfying the individual taste of each reader can be hazardous, especially if you are not acquainted with that person. One reader will react very favorably to a breezy, conversational writing style, while another will think it phony or too chummy. Customer A will accept "It's too bad we mixed up your last two orders," while Customer B will think the phrase "It's too bad" sarcastic.

In any event, your relationship to your reader will usually determine the tone and style of your letter. This is why you will rarely write the same letter to two different people even though the subject is identical. Let's take an example. Suppose you're in charge of purchasing for your company. For years you have been a friend of Stephen R. Gaines, the sales manager for a supplier you buy from. Somehow you failed to place an order for Widgets, and you're nearly out of stock. A big problem with back orders looms if you don't get a shipment at once. Good old Gaines comes through by giving you overnight service at considerable sacrifice. In expressing your appreciation, you might say something like this:

> Dear Steve:
>
> The 600 Widgets were here this morning when I got to work, and I still don't believe it. I won't ask how you managed it, but you really saved my skin. The next time we get together, *I'll* pick up the tab.
>
> Steve, thanks.

If the same special service had been given by another supplier—someone you are not personally acquainted with—you would be equally grateful. But your expression of gratitude is likely to be something along this line:

> Dear Mr. Taylor:
>
> I appreciate very much your prompt shipment of the 600 Widgets I ordered earlier this week. They arrived this morning, immediately after we shipped out our last half dozen to one of our best customers. Thank you for the special attention you gave the order.

The above examples show why you can't write by formula. While the ingredients are basically the same, the tone and style are quite different. The success of your letters, then, depends on (1) the situation, (2) who the reader is, and (3) your relationship with that reader.

YOUR TURN

Assume that you recently attended a business convention where you met an old college friend who is now product development manager for an electronics firm that specializes in minicomputers. During your brief chat, your friend promised to send you just-released information on a new desk computer, Giant Lilliput, in which you are very much interested.

After two weeks you have received nothing from your friend, and you decide to write a reminder that you are still eager to have information about the Giant Lilliput.

Read the following letter and then write your own. (As you plan your letter, visualize a person with whom you were somewhat closely associated in college but haven't seen since you both were graduated.) You will find a suggested letter on page 203.

> Dear T. R.:
>
> Just a reminder that you promised to send me information on the Giant Lilliput about which we spoke in Minneapolis in April.
>
> Very truly yours,

Make Your Letters Human

In our previous discussions of report writing, we talked a great deal about avoiding stuffy language. "Say it simply" is also good advice when you're writing a letter. Some people assume an entirely different character when they sit down to dictate a letter. Perhaps they feel vulnerable when they attempt to be themselves. Or they may believe that every letter is a contract, with possibly nasty legal implications. Or simply that a "learned-sounding" communication awes and impresses readers.

It is true that some people are suspicious of writers who try to dazzle them with slick charm and old-pal language. And well they might be. We, too, have an aversion to oily inanities that reek of hard sell. Yet it is safe to say that nearly all successful correspondents are people who can exhibit a personal warmth in their letters without sounding like hucksters. If there is one most important ingredient in a business letter, aside from accuracy and clarity, it would have to be personal warmth.

Of course, you can't approach every letter-writing situation with unbounded joy and good cheer. Some letters are necessarily impersonal—contract proposals, for example. Others are barely civil: the last of a dozen attempts to collect an old bill or a third response to a nagging and thoroughly unprincipled critic, for example. Still, for most writers, the need for reserved-in-tone or ugly letters is pretty rare.

Although a few people you correspond with may prefer a to-whom-it-may-concern letter, most like warmth and friendliness. Look at the following:

> Dear Sir:
> Pursuant to your request for information about quantity discounts on the Galaxy Electronic Reminder, the enclosed schedule provides complete information on this company's discount policy.
> Hoping this schedule will satisfy your requirements, we are
> Yours truly,

The foregoing is not as rare as you might think. A lot of people write like that, presumably donning their Scrooge uniform just before they start to dictate. Let's see what's wrong:

1. There is every reason to use the addressee's name in the salutation when you know it. "Dear Ms. (when you don't know a woman's marital status) Rowan" or "Dear Mr. Ramsing" is much better.

2. The writer used only one personal pronoun— *we*—and even that one is not convincing. There is nothing wrong with using *I* frequently in most of your letters; indeed there really is no substitute for that personal pronoun if you want your letters to convey sincerity.

3. Hackneyed phrases like "Pursuant to" have a way of destroying individuality in letters. Here are others you will want to avoid: *herewith enclosed, under separate cover, with reference to your request, in reply to your request, in accordance with your wishes, acknowledging your request for information, in reply to yours of the 14th would state,* and *please advise.*

   Also beware of "ing" closings like the one illustrated. They require you to wind up with such inanities as *I am, We are, we remain,* etc.

4. "Yours truly" is considered a poor closing for any letter, although the reason is obscure. If you want to be formal, you can use "Yours very truly" or "Very truly yours"; and if you need to show deep respect, "Respectfully yours." But for most letters, warmer closings such as "Sincerely yours" and "Cordially yours" or simply "Sincerely" or "Cordially" are preferred.

Now let's look at a personal response to the person who inquired about the Galaxy Electronic Reminder.

> Dear Mr. Ramsing:
> I've enclosed a schedule of our quantity discounts on the Galaxy Electronic Reminder. Please note that we offer a 35 percent trade discount on all orders regardless of quantity.
> I am delighted that you are interested in this revolutionary executive aid. We guarantee same-day shipment of every order.
> Sincerely yours,

Your Turn

See what you can do to bring some warmth to the following to-whom-it-may-concern letter; then check yours with that on page 203.

> Dear Madam:
> With reference to your inquiry concerning your account balance, it has been discovered that credit was not recorded for your payment of $64.88, check dated September 3, since it was received after statements were mailed.
> Trusting that you have not been inconvenienced at this oversight, I am,
> Yours truly,

Deal with the Subject at Hand

It is surprising how many letter writers fail to provide the specific information asked for by a correspondent. If a customer asks when an order can be shipped and what the terms of payment are, you won't produce a successful letter if you don't deal with both questions. Too often, writers dictate their responses without really having read the letter they are responding to. The best way to assure yourself of not overlooking anything is to underline on the incoming letter (or make marginal notations about) the points that need to be covered in a response.

Following is an example of a writer's not paying attention to the questions that were asked. A lady purchased a ring-binder cookbook several years ago from a mail-order house. Through constant use the binder has fallen apart, and she writes to ask whether she can obtain a new one.

Dear Mrs. Loftin:

I am sorry we cannot replace your cookbook, which you purchased from us in 1977. That particular book was superseded by a new edition (see flyer enclosed), and there is no stock on hand of the old one.

Sincerely yours,

Although the writer was apologetic, the lady's question was not answered. She wants to know whether a replacement *binder* can be purchased for her much-used cookbook. If the writer had really studied the incoming letter, he might have produced something like this:

Dear Mrs. Loftin:

When we purchased the first edition of *Bertha Fairchild's Easy Cookbook* from the publisher, we did not order extra binders and thus never had a reserve stock. And the binder for the second edition (see the enclosed brochure) is smaller than yours, so there's no solution there.

The manufacturer of the binders (Croft Manufacturers, 111 South Broad Street, Philadelphia 19102) probably has the size you need or can refer you to a local stationer who carries them. Although it's not likely that you can get the original binder, a blank one might do just as well.

Thank you for writing—and good luck!

Cordially yours,

Stress the Positive

Some people think in terms of what *can't* be done instead of what *can,* and this attitude spills over into their writing.

Dear Miss Jethro:

Unfortunately, we've had difficulty keeping a sufficient supply of the Chilton Coffee Bar to satisfy the unexpected demand, and right now we're about three weeks behind in our back orders.

It looks now like we'll not be able to make shipment of the four bars you ordered until September 9. I am sorry if this will inconvenience you.

Yours sincerely,

The writer of the above was thinking negatively. Note the opening, "Unfortunately, we've had difficulty keeping a sufficient supply. . . ." Most people with sales responsibilities would be delighted to experience a situation where demand exceeds supply. And there's something to be said for the customer's good taste in choosing an article that is so popular.

"It looks now like we'll not be able to make shipment . . . until September 9" is also negative. Although we don't think you should deliberately mask the truth, neither do we believe you have to tear your hair out in despair when you face such a situation.

Compare the foregoing with the following.

Dear Miss Jethro:

I'm glad to have your order for four Chilton Coffee Bars. It's a very popular item—so popular, in fact, that we can't seem to keep enough in stock to fill all orders immediately.

We can, though, make shipment by September 9. I'd like to do better and will if I can. In any event, I'm convinced that you'll think the Chilton Coffee Bar was worth a short wait.

Very cordially yours,

YOUR TURN

Rewrite the following statements so that they are more positive. Suggested answers are on pages 203-204.

1. We can't ship your modular office units until we receive from you the color you require.

2. I'm sorry the contracts will not be ready to mail before the end of next week.

3. If you had written to me directly, this mix-up would not have occurred.

4. Unfortunately, we had to substitute Model 3K for the Model 4B that you ordered. The price is no higher. If you don't like Model 3K, please advise.

5. The unfortunate truckers' strike prevented our making shipment before this. I know you had planned to feature these organs in your Christmas promotion. I hope a December 3 shipping date—which appears a certainty now that the strike is over—won't be too big a disappointment.

Use the Right Timing

Generally speaking, you should try to answer within two days those letters that require a response. Sometimes, of course, it is impossible to do so. You may not have the information you need, or you're away from the office, or you simply have so many pressures that you're behind with your correspondence.

When a sales opportunity is involved or good public relations is a critical issue, you should try at least to acknowledge correspondence you receive, telling the sender when a more specific response can be expected. For example:

Dear Mrs. Henderson:

I've been in touch with the manufacturer about delivery of the Clarion Sound Lectern in time for your April 12 MENC convention in Miami Beach. The hold-up appears to be in the factory where the cabinets are made. I'm to get a firm commitment—one way or the other—by March 11, and just as soon as I do I'll call or write you.

I'm optimistic. For one thing, we'll keep the heat on at this end. Then, too, this particular manufacturer has never let us down before.

Thank you for your patience.

Sincerely,

There are times, however, when a prompt response is not advisable. If that sounds strange, consider these situations:

1. You receive a job application from a person whose letter and résumé indicate that he does not have the qualifications for the position applied for.
2. A letter comes from a new ad agency in town in which the owner proposes that you dump your present agency and switch your business to her.
3. An organization called Americans for Human Decency writes a bitter diatribe against your company about its policy of placing advertising in what the organization calls "indecent" publications.

Nearly every business organization gets "problem" letters such as those described. An overnight response is likely to evoke the suspicion that you gave little (if any) thought to the writer's proposal. It is often best in such situations to let the matter lie dormant for several days before responding. Even though you may feel inclined to zip off a quick negative response, a reasonable wait will suggest that you gave the proposal a good deal of thought, whether you actually did or not.

Let's say you are responding to the man who applied for a position that he is not qualified for. After a few days' wait, you might answer the letter like this:

Dear Mr. Wallin:
I appreciate having your application for the position of controller, which we recently advertised in *The Wall Street Journal.*
Over 100 people responded to our ad, many of whom were extremely well qualified, so it was a difficult choice for us to make. Although you were not selected, I do want to thank you for your interest in our organization.
Yours cordially,

Say No Gently

Often you will have to say no to people to whom you write—solicitations for donations, unreasonable requests, and the like. Your mission in responding is to do the least amount of damage possible—indeed to keep on good terms with your correspondent, if possible. This is not easy; no one likes to be turned down. But remember that nine times out of ten, the situation that requires you to say no arises out of innocent ignorance on the part of your correspondent. So no matter how unreasonable the request, hold your temper.

Sometimes there may be two or more favors asked in the same letter. If you are in a position to grant one of them, start there. In other words, first say what you *can* do and then say what you *can't* do. For example:

Dear Mr. Krantz:
I'm pleased to send you our annual report for the years 1980 and 1981.
Unfortunately, the reports for the years 1970-1979, which you asked for, are not available except on microfilm. If you are in this area, you are welcome to view these reports, which are housed in our library.
Sincerely,

If you can do nothing for your correspondent, you have to say no fairly quickly. Yet you can often salvage a friendship if you (1) are tactful and sympathetic and (2) give reasons why you can't comply.

Dear Professor LeGrand:

I am delighted, of course, at your interest in our company magazine, *Panorama*. The two latest issues are enclosed.

I am sorry I cannot put you on the mailing list to receive this publication regularly, Professor LeGrand. Because of the demand for it by outside-the-company friends, we were forced to establish a policy limiting distribution to our employees. I am sure you understand that the expense of printing and postage plus the cost of maintaining a large mailing list represent a greater investment than we feel we can justify.

Nevertheless, it is gratifying to know that people like you think so highly of *Panorama*. You were thoughtful to applaud our efforts.

Sincerely yours,

Your Turn

Assume that you are advertising manager for a firm in Grand Rapids that manufactures and sells institutional furniture for schools and colleges. Every year, you receive several requests from high school and college yearbook editors, asking you to place an ad in the yearbook "since our school buys from your firm."

Evaluate the following response to these letters; then write your own version. Use whatever reasons you think appropriate for turning down the request. (A suggested letter is on page 204.)

Dear _____:

Since it is impossible for our firm to advertise in every high school and college yearbook, I must reject your request. Company policy is that we advertise only in such publications in the community of Grand Rapids.

Yours truly,

Do a Little More than You Have To

When you cannot satisfy the requests of your correspondents, often you can refer them to someone who can or put some extra effort into helping. A little extra legwork can win friends and influence people. Compare:

Dear Mr. Wardman:

Our company does not manufacture calculator-clocks; therefore, we cannot fill your order.

Yours very truly,

Dear Mr. Wardman:

Thank you for your order for six Regent calculator-clocks.

Our company makes only clocks used in appliances and automobiles, Mr. Wardman, and I'm afraid we can't serve you directly. My list of suppliers shows that the Regent calculator-clock is manufactured and distributed by Kinkaid Corporation, 300 South 36 Street, Omaha, Nebraska 68131. I know they'll be happy to help you.

Cordially yours,

YOUR TURN

The Academy of Design, a group of design consultants in Chicago, often receives applications for admission from people who are under the impression that the firm is an educational institution.

Following is the response written to these applicants:

Dear _____:

Since we are not an educational institution (we offer consulting services to business and government organizations), we must decline your application for admission.

Sincerely yours,

Prepare an appropriate response to such inquiries. Then compare your letter with the one on page 204.

Confirm Important Agreements by Letter

When you make oral agreements that involve technical matters and, more important, a good deal of money, it is usually wise to confirm each agreement by letter. Here, specificity is all-important. Memories are short, and people sometimes forget (or pretend to forget) what they agreed to.

Let's say you are responsible for making arrangements for a companywide sales conference at Matador Manor, a resort hotel on the Gulf Coast. You have visited the Matador and talked at length with the general manager about the number of residence rooms you need and the rate, the meeting rooms you require, audiovisual aids to be provided, food services such as special group luncheons and dinners, transportation to and from the airport, recreation facilities to be provided, method of handling gratuities, how payment is to be made, and so on.

You will want to put in a letter the specific details of what you think was agreed upon. If you don't, it is possible that some of the services you understood were to be provided were not, in fact, in the hotel manager's plans. It doesn't matter, actually, who writes the letter—you or the hotel manager (some hotels have fill-in contracts covering agreements with clients)—but there ought to be a written confirmation.

Important oral sales and purchasing agreements are often put in writing. In the letter that follows, the writer has talked with a manufacturer about placing an order for Atlas metric socket wrench sets and now follows up the discussion with a confirmation letter.

IMPORTS UNLIMITED
2800 Fairview Avenue
Boise, Idaho 83706

October 24, 19--

Mr. David R. Benjamin, Vice President
Ebersole Manufacturing Company
1600 Oak Brook Road
Hinsdale, Illinois 60521

Dear Mr. Benjamin:

This letter will confirm the specifications for Atlas metric socket wrench sets that we discussed October 17.

Contents of the Set

The set includes the following:

1. One 1/4" drive--6 pt., with one each of the following sockets: 3, 4, 4.5, 5, 5.5, 6, 7, and 8 mm

2. One 3/8" drive--12 pt., with one each of the following sockets: 9, 10, 11, 12, 14, 17, and 19 mm

3. One 21 mm spark plug socket, with an 8" reversible ratchet handle

4. One 3" and one 6" extension

5. One 3/8" and one 1/4" adapter

6. One 6" and 1/4" drive spinner handle

7. One metal (steel) tool box for the above

Specifications

You guarantee the following specifications:

1. All tools exceed federal specifications #GGG--2641d for test load strength and hardness.

2. All tools are chrome-plated and heat-forged of chrome-moly steel.

3. All tools are engineered for precision fit--tolerances conform to American Standard Code A5AB182.

Warranty

All tools are warranted against defects in material and workmanship. Any tool lacking in quality and durability may be returned to you for free replacement.

Price

The list price of each Atlas metric socket wrench set is $13.98, less a trade discount of 15 percent, in quantities of 200 sets or more. In quantities less than 200, the price per set is $15.60, less a trade discount of 15 percent. An additional cash discount of 3 percent is given on all orders when payment is received by you within 15 days of the date of the invoice.

Delivery and Shipping Charges

Delivery is guaranteed at our place of business Boise within 10 days of receipt of order. Shipping charges will be paid by the purchaser.

If the above is in accord with your understanding, please sign in the space provided below and return the original to me.

Very truly yours,

B.R. Mathies

B. R. Mathies
Director of Purchasing

Accepted _____

Date _____

The foregoing is essentially a legal document; thus the language is somewhat formal. Note the use of headings and enumerations for easy reference.

You will see that the recipient, David R. Benjamin, is asked to sign the letter (he will receive the original and one copy) and return the signed original to the writer.

HIGHLIGHTS OF CHAPTER 13

Following are seven basic guidelines for effective letter writing:

1. Make your letters human.
2. Deal with the subject at hand.
3. Stress the positive.
4. Use the right timing.
5. Say no gently.
6. Do a little more than you have to.
7. Confirm important agreements by letter.

A final word

Unlike certain wines and other spirits, writers don't always improve with age. Experience may help some, but experience alone doesn't guarantee proficiency in anything—especially writing. And the main reason that most writers don't get a lot better as they churn out more and more reports is that they are too easily satisfied with their work.

The ability to be self-critical often separates the amateur from the professional. When a pro golfer is slicing or hooking or putting badly, he asks himself, What am I doing wrong? When he finds out, he works on the fault until it is corrected. Whether it's golf, tennis, or running the marathon, you can't win if you don't constantly undergo self-evaluation.

Did you ever know a copy editor? He or she (usually the latter) is the person whom the publisher relies on to make sure the authors' work will reflect credit on them as well as the publisher. She can be stubborn, even downright cranky, about correctness and clarity in writing, and she is generally given full authority to fix sentence faults, bad logic and non sequiturs, rambling paragraphs, disconnected ideas, misused words, overwriting, circumlocution, and errors in capitalization, punctuation, spelling, dates, names, and so on. In short, she's a faultfinder, which often makes her the author's nemesis. No matter, she delights in her role as "protector of language purity." The publisher doesn't give her much credit, even though she saves many authors from oblivion, but she is indispensable.

From this point on, we'd like you to think of yourself as an editor—a highly critical evaluator of everything you put on paper. When you get in the habit of ruthlessly slashing your own copy, rewriting it, then slashing it again, and patiently rewriting a third time, you're on your way to becoming an effective business writer. If you're really serious, you might even ask others to comment on the reports they receive from you. Whether you agree with your critics or not, you're bound to learn something. If, that is, you keep an open mind.

Good luck!

Solutions to exercises

The following solutions are merely suggested. In most cases there are equally effec-tive ways of handling the problem.

Page 10

I think the problem can easily be solved by allowing each department manager to have his or her own petty cash fund of, say, $100. This would make it easy to buy the special supplies needed without having to go through Purchasing.

Page 19

When you buy a machine, be sure to pick the one that does the job best.

Page 20

1. Since our capital is limited, each investment should be made on the basis of its potential profit.

2. Please make sure that each travel-expense item can be justified.

3. The forecast is for rain, so we may have to hold our meeting inside.

4. Can the new policy be put into effect by March 1?

5. Spirit duplicating is the least expensive method of printing the newsletter.

Page 21

Our first aim, then, is to get the greatest productivity at the least cost. This should not be hard to do if there is good management, and it can result in higher profits without affecting morale.

Page 24

1. Here is the report on fleet truck rentals that you asked for April 17.

2. We have received Ramco's bid for constructing the Modesto distribution center.

3. May I have your recommendations by May 5?

4. If you approve of this proposal, please sign below.

5. I especially want to thank the Personnel Department staff for their cooperation.

6. The Salary Review Committee will meet Tuesday at 10:00 a.m.

7. As I said before, it is especially important to solve this problem quickly.

8. Please staple the pages so that they won't get lost.

Page 25

My principal suggestion for upgrading sales representatives and providing better opportunities for advancement is a revised incentive compensation plan. This plan, which would be based on individual performance, is described in this report.

Pages 25–26

1. When you are analyzing quality for the sake of improving it, you should work toward eliminating errors rather than simply finding and correcting them.
2. It makes no sense for the industry to establish new manufacturing standards until we look at the results of the research.
3. A second way to reduce noise is to install muted bells on telephones in rooms where there are many instruments in constant use.
4. When you deal with factory workers, follow this rule: praise in public and censure in private.
5. When you set up an organization chart, make sure that reporting lines are clear to every employee.
6. We expect over 200,000 responses to our questionnaire. Since our computer equipment is already being used at full capacity, we'll have to get the tabulating done elsewhere. There is probably a time-sharing installation that can do the job for us.

Page 29

Records should be retained for two main reasons:

1. For information needed by employees
2. For information required by the government, banks, and others who ask for it

But records serve two other purposes: source material for a company history and training material for executives. Thus every department in the company should retain certain records.

Page 31

Here is the report on shrink-wrapping that you requested August 17. You will note that there are three sections—Requirements, Methods, and Cost. I am sending a copy of the report to each member of the Systems Group.

Page 32

1. Although there were many problems in switching to cycle billing, the system is now working smoothly.
2. Staggering starting and quitting times did cause some inconvenience at first, but everyone seems content with the plan now.

Pages 33–34

1. Even though the carton was clearly marked "Perishable," it remained for three days on the loading dock.
2. On her wrist, each hostess wore a silk band on which the word "Welcome" was printed in blue and yellow.

3. When flying on company business, employees will be authorized to book first-class seats only on transatlantic or transpacific flights.

Page 34

Promoting and selling the company's product is a marketing function, while developing a favorable company image is a public relations function. However, these functions often overlap between the two departments.

Page 36

I was pleased to have reports from both you and Ms. Bailey.

Pages 36–37

1. Hodgkins is as successful as anyone else in collecting overdue accounts—probably more successful.

2. Opportunities for women are greater in the Waltham Corporation than in any other corporation in our entire industry.

3. The focus of these studies has been on the reduction of turnover.

Pages 37-40

SOLUTION

WORLDWIDE DISTRIBUTORS INC.

Comments

Interoffice Memorandum

TO: Mrs. Cynthia Townsend   FROM: C. L. Bates
DEPT.:   Personnel   DEPT.: Personnel
SUBJECT: A New-Employee Induction   DATE: March 15, 19—
         Program

Dear Cynthia:

Here is the report you asked for on a new-employee induction program for Worldwide. In it I have reviewed the present procedure, described the need for change, and presented a proposal for a new procedure.

This paragraph is easier to read because it is broken down into two sentences.

PRESENT PROCEDURE

As you know, our present procedure for inducting new employees is brief and highly informal. One of us in Personnel gives employees a quick welcome, hands them a copy of "Worldwide's World," and escorts them to the departments where they will work. There really is no program.

Again, the sentence is too long. Notice how much more effective the paragraph is when it is broken down into three sentences.

NEED FOR CHANGE

With the rapid growth of the company, it becomes more and more difficult for employees to learn about our various products, the markets we serve, the firm's objectives and future plans—in other words, who we are and what we do. There is no opportunity for new employees to meet top

In the original memorandum, the writer has a 120-word sentence! No matter how well-written a report is, readers are bound to get lost if they

executives, learn about interdepartmental relationships, and find out how their own department fits into the total picture. Finally, there is the matter of educating employees about such things as compensation, retirement, fringe benefits, and general company policies.

All the things mentioned are important not only in avoiding costly errors but also from the standpoint of general morale—the sense of belonging and pride in being a part of the organization.

A NEW PROGRAM PROPOSAL

To overcome the weaknesses of the present procedure, I propose that we establish a formal two-day induction program for all new employees.

Frequency

The program would be staged twice a month—possibly the first and the fifteenth. Since new employees are hired daily, many would be placed on the job before going through the program. This is unavoidable. Indeed, this might be an advantage. Employees would have had an opportunity to get their bearings and thus be more receptive to formal induction.

Major Topics

The major topics featured in the program might be the folowing:
Company history—a brief account of the beginnings of Worldwide, its growth patterns, and its principal "shakers and movers."

Products—a presentation of our products and services, with emphasis on markets served and our position in the market.

Organization—the present structure of Worldwide, including the setup of major divisions and how they interrelate.

Personnel policies—compensation, promotions and transfers, vacations, working hours, pay advances, sick leave, retirement plan, insurance, and various personnel services.

Employee activities—recreation, hobby groups, in-company and outside educational programs.

Special help—who to see in the company for special assistance on personal problems, legal and tax assistance, medical attention, etc.

General Structure

Each program would be planned so that:
1. It is of maximum interest and inspiration. Extensive use would be made of audiovisual devices (motion pictures, overhead projectors, tapes, flip charts, etc.).

2. Wherever possible, top executives would be asked to participate, but selected "firing line" employees would also be invited.

are not allowed a pause occasionally. Notice in the solution that there are now four sentences instead of one. Also, a new paragraph has been provided. These simple changes help to make the report much easier to read and understand.

In the original memorandum, sentences two and four are fragments. The sixth sentence is a run-on.

Notice in the original memorandum that the copy under the heading A NEW PROGRAM PROPOSAL is solid. The reader is entitled to a "visual break" (white space). You will see that the copy is much easier to read when it is broken up.

In the original memorandum, the word *principle* is incorrect.

Notice how the addition of headings and the special display of the material makes these major topics easier to grasp.

In the original version, the word *personal* is incorrect.

Look at the paragraph in the original memorandum beginning, "Each program would be . . ." A connective is needed in the second sentence *(but)*. In the third sentence, the reference is vague. Who is insisting? These two problems have been corrected in the revised version at the left.

3. Every participant would be carefully instructed on how to prepare the presentation. We would insist that there be no long speeches and instead brief, interesting "show-and-tell" presentations.

4. To the greatest extent possible, we would give the new employees a chance to participate (that is, those who have been on the job for a week or two.)

THE FIRST STEP

If you think this general proposal has merit, I suggest that you ask to appear before the Executive Committee and the Operations Committee (meeting jointly) to present the plan. At this meeting each division executive might be asked to appoint a representative to serve on a special Employee Induction Program Committee. The purpose of this group would be to assist in the initial planning and then to serve as a standing committee to help manage the program.

FURTHER DISCUSSION

Please let me know if you wish to discuss this idea further. I have obtained several articles and booklets on induction programs that you might like to see.

Sincerely,
C. L. B.

In the original memorandum, the first sentence under the heading **THE FIRST STEP** is awkwardly constructed. The one at the left is much clearer. Notice also in this paragraph that there are now three sentences instead of two.

Notice that *serving* in the original version has been changed to *to serve* so that the wording will be parallel with *to assist*.

The sentences under the heading **FURTHER DISCUSSION** have been rewritten for clarity.

Pages 41–42

1. An error in the inventory will lead to other erroneous figures in the balance sheet, such as total current assets, total assets, owner's equity, and the total of liabilities and owner's equity. It will also affect key figures in the income statement. Among these are the cost of merchandise sold, the gross profit on sales, and the net income for the period.

2. The title of the statistical table should be centered at the top and as short as possible. If you need several words to identify the table, use a subtitle.

3. Almost any business can increase its sales if it does not consider the cost of selling. Obviously, this is not realistic. As a matter of fact, in many companies profit on sales is estimated before the sales are made.

4. The carrier, according to the contract printed on the back of the bill of lading, is responsible for losses of or damages to merchandise. In the case of the Hooper shipment, damage amounts to about $3500.

5. Although fatigue and boredom both contribute to absenteeism, lack of incentive is also an important factor.

6. The revenue that is derived from sales taxes is used in many different ways.

7. Because we believe that production costs can be greatly reduced, we now use computers to handle many operations that used to be done manually.

8. Statistics can be used in hundreds of ways—for example, locating new markets, determining population trends, making decisions concerning production quantities, comparing wages and prices, and deciding on new branch-store locations.

9a. The production of energy-efficient heating systems is a project to which our engineers have given and are giving much time and thought.

b. Our Tarrytown plant produces more Widgets a year than any of our other plants.

10. In our warehouses is a wide variety of electronic equipment.

Page 46

1. It is difficult to achieve full agreement between the people in publicity, PR, and promotion and those reponsible for collections.

2. In her remarks about opportunities, Arlene emphasized the history of sex discrimination in this company.

3. I don't think the disagreement between the Accounting and Marketing departments is as serious as Zazzera believes it is.

4. Employees have different opinions about the new corporate logo, most of them negative.

5. Although the method proposed by Personnel has merit, I think it stops short of a real solution to the problem.

Page 48

I have learned from three of our major suppliers (Wenco, Ramsey, and Consolidated) that there is likely to be a shortage of copper wire by the end of the year because of a prolonged strike in the industry. It might be a good idea to place a large order now so that we'll be sure of having the wire we need. What do you think?

Page 51

Unless one is calling on customers nearly every day, it is hard to understand the importance of good design in selling our products. I agree that effective design is expensive, but it is an absolute necessity.

Page 52

I like many things about the proposed new job application form. However, I have some suggestions that I think will help make the form even easier for applicants to fill out.

Page 53

1. I agree with Loftin about using commercial transportation where possible. However, we should keep in mind that many places can only be reached by car.

2. I believe that if we had had final specifications earlier, the packaging problem would have been solved by now.

3. I cannot accept the reasons Russell gave for exceeding the entertainment budget in April by 30 percent.

4. Although the shipping delay was apparently unavoidable, it cost us a big order.

5. The recruiting manager's record in filling personnel requisitions is admirable.

Page 54

1. Our sales performance in November is not encouraging.

2. As in July and August, there were several computer errors in September customer billings.

3. I think it is unfortunate that the purchasing manager did not follow our recommendations.

4. I believe that our present retirement program is inadequate.

5. It is especially important that our company, which specializes in graphics, produce annual reports that are models for the industry.

Pages 56–57

At the conclusion of the audit, the internal auditor will submit a written report identifying the objective and scope of the study, the methods used, and the findings. The report should show not only the number, percent, and type of errors, but also include the auditor's recommendations for improvement. Remember, the auditor's job is to advise supervisors of their shortcomings. And it is the responsibility of each supervisor to follow through once any shortcomings have been pointed out.

Pages 68–69

1a. We think our advertising campaign was very successful and helped pave the way for more effective personal selling.

b. It is important that systems analysts find out exactly what management's needs are before deciding on the input to be recorded.

2a. It seems to me that some of our secretarial employees would benefit from a refresher course in English grammar.

b. The cost of the new corporate logo was much less than reported by the art director's staff.

3. It seems to me that we should be cautious about moving too fast on acquisitions, for in our eagerness to grow we could get hurt.

4a. On the basis of my research, I would recommend Northbrook as the location of a new distribution center in the Chicago area.

b. It would appear that four distributors offered higher discounts to dealers than our policy allows.

5. Sales to the Canadian market in the third quarter this year were 20 percent over the same period last year—a very good showing indeed.

6. Factory absenteeism on Monday, the 24th, was up 11 percent. It's possible that "Super Sunday" (the 23d) had something to do with it.

7. Errors in the Inspection Department in the first quarter of this year were reduced 7 percent over the same period last year—certainly an improvement.

8. Is it possible that some of the new suppliers serving this market could give us better quality and prices than we are now getting?

9. Like some of our other competitors, Peterson is sometimes inclined to put profits above everything else.

10. Let's not forget that the only reason the Personnel Department exists is to provide service to all our employees.

11. From Clausen's comment, I deduce that she thinks we have not been discreet in handling confidential credit information.

12. Before a work measurement program is begun, all supervisors should be thoroughly briefed. They must have a good understanding of it if they are expected to cooperate. Supervisors must also be in a position to explain and help to sell the program to the clerical people reporting to them. Secretaries are key people too. They must know as much as their bosses and help them put the idea across to others.

Page 74

1. Inadequacy of present typewriters

   a. Old and in poor condition
   b. Difficult to get efficient production
   c. Cost (in terms of time)
   d. Poor quality of communications

2. Why electronic typewriters?

   a. Increased production
   b. Better-looking communications to stockholders
   c. Improved attitude of typists (turnover reduction)

3. Cost of electronics

   a. Trade-in allowance for old typewriters (mention expected useful life of the old ones is two years maximum)
   b. Can get special price on this year's model (next year's model is ready for release)

4. Recommendations

Page 80

TO: R. J. Hillyer
SUBJECT: Bottlenecks in the Shipping Department

At your request I spent the week of January 3 investigating the conditions in the Shipping Department. Here is a report of my findings.

You know, of course, that there is a serious problem in Shipping. Right now the company has a two-week backlog of unfilled orders. Some customers have canceled their orders, and others are angrily protesting. On the basis of what I found out, I would say that the problem there is essentially *people,* and this is where I'll start.

PEOPLE

Etc.

Page 87

<h2 style="text-align:center">MONTHLY MILEAGE REPORT</h2>

District Office _____   Date _____

Name of Representative	Miles Driven		Variance (Explain +'s below)
	This Month	Last Month	
Totals			

Explanations: _____

_____

(Several horizontal lines for explanations)

Prepared by _____

Page 108

The personnel director suggested that to avoid traffic jams in the early morning and late afternoon, the company stagger the beginning and closing times.

Page 112

1. The use of an outside consultant in methods improvement is highly attractive, mainly because employees find it difficult to deal objectively with sacred cows or in fact to remedy procedural bottlenecks.

2. The main objective of the accounts payable function is to keep accurate records of amounts owed to creditors and to make payments when they are due.

Pages 112-113

1a. The principal purpose in offering credit is to increase sales.

b. Six members of the Suggestion Committee were at the meeting.

c. New employees receive one week's vacation the first year.

d. I have decided to eliminate two of the five marketing channels we now use.

e. The company attorney recommended additional liability insurance.

f. The Manufacturing Committee proposed a complete revision of the piece-rate wage plan because the present one is unfair.

2a. The initial mark-on is the difference between the cost and the original price of the merchandise, regardless of the price at which the merchandise is sold.

b. The Budget Committee should include the president, merchandise managers, chief accountant, treasurer, and director of personnel.

c. Language training is perhaps the most important part of the orientation program for overseas people, especially those who come in close contact with foreign nationals.

3. Many believe that high-speed computer equipment is not necessary for operations research studies. Useful results can be obtained with mathematical techniques. Yet computers can save time in solving formulas, developing data, and analyzing data to show relationships.

4. To whom should the R&D manager report? There are several possibilities—the vice president for finance, marketing, product planning, research, and manufacturing, for example. I think, however, this person should report directly to the president.

5. We must keep in mind what makes a good company handbook for employees. It must be brief. It must be simple. And it must be visually exciting.

6. Most employees make suggestions for one primary reason: to contribute their ideas. The possibility of earning a cash award is secondary.

7. When we asked the two warehouse workers why they were taking the canned hams, they gave a surprising answer: the company expects them to help themselves!

Pages 126-127

RECOMMENDATIONS

I recommend the following steps to strengthen our community relations.

1. Develop a VIP Mailing List.   A mailing list of civic-thought leaders and all identifiable members of the local power structure would be highly useful. It would be used to distribute information concerning such things as the company's position on labor disputes, price increases, expansion plans, pollution standards, and corporate giving.

2. Build and Maintain Good Media Relations.   It is important that the local media—press, radio, and television—get, to the maximum degree possible, what they want, when they want it. These people should be supplied with the home telephone numbers of designated executives who can speak officially for the company.

3. Do More Institutional Advertising.   Institutional advertising in all three media can be very powerful as an image builder. The community should know what we are doing in support of local projects—for example, the Bordentown Symphony.

4. Organize a Speakers' Bureau.   A speakers' bureau could, I think, provide a fine service to the community. Such a service would, of course, be free and made available to schools and colleges, civic organizations, youth and senior citizens groups, and others.

5. Participate Actively in Local Groups.   It is important that the company be fully represented in such organizations as the Chamber of Commerce, Lions, Kiwanis, Rotary, and similar groups; and such professional organizations as the Society for the Advancement of Management, American Society of Chemical Engineers, American Marketing Association, Advertising Club, and Business and Professional Women.

Page 139

INCENTIVE PLANS

Many different types of incentive plans have been devised over the years. First, I will mention six of the early ones that received considerable attention but were abandoned one by one. Then I will describe in detail the plan that is most widely used today—the Standard-Hour Plan.

Early Incentive Plans

1. The Halsey Plan. The Halsey Plan provided. . . .
2. The Bedeaux Plan. This plan also. . . .
3. The Haynes Plan. The Haynes Plan provided. . . .
4. The Rowan Plan. This plan was based on a. . . .
4. The Emerson Plan. The Emerson Plan was similar to. . . .
6. The Gantt Plan. This plan provided. . . .

The Standard-Hour Plan

The most widely used incentive plan in use today is the Standard-Hour Plan. Because of its popularity, it merits a full description, along with a discussion of its outstanding features.

Description. The Standard-Hour Plan requires that time standards be set as accurately as possible. Then, as workers complete units of production, they . . .

Outstanding Features. The most important feature of the Standard-Hour Plan is that it is fair. Workers say that they can easily understand the "mechanics" and that the plan provides a strong incentive. Not to be overlooked, however . . .

Pages 139-140

2. Although the straight-line method of depreciation was used on all office furniture and equipment, the annual rate of depreciation varied from item to item. Following are three examples.

Item	Original Value ($)	Annual Depreciation ($)	Annual Rate of Depreciation (%)
Desk computer	3100	248	8
Filing equipment	2720	272	10
Secretarial desk	325	75	15

3a. $76,600, $43,500, $61,400, $53,800, $49,300, $66,200

b. In a recent poll, about 63 percent of the employees indicated a preference for the earlier starting hour, but only about 27 percent favored a thirty-minute lunch. Of the 615 employees who drive to work, about half indicated difficulty in finding parking space.

4. Our accounts receivable as of September 30 appear to be in good condition. Nearly 90 percent are either not yet due or less than thirty one days past due. Only 2 percent are overdue by ninety days.

5a. circle   **b.** bar   **c.** line

6a. Second level
b. First level
c. Fourth level
d. Third level

Page 144

A rough *first* statement of purpose might be as follows:

To provide information to the Senior Staff Committee on the need for a company library, its functions, start-up and operating costs, location and layout, operating procedures, and staffing requirements.

A revised, complete statement of purpose will be found on page 000.

Page 148

A proposed outline follows:

PURPOSE

THE PAST RECORD

    Number and Types of Accidents
    Cause
    Responsibility
    Extent of Injury
    Cost to the Company

ELEMENTS OF A SUCCESSFUL SAFETY PROGRAM

    Role of Top Management
    Establishment and Enforcement of Rules

Training Programs
Employee Participation
Employment of a Safety Director
Measurement of Safety Performance

COMPARATIVE COSTS

Cost of Present Losses
Cost of New Program

RECOMMENDATIONS

PURPOSE

The unusually large number of accidents in the factory of Crown Manufacturing Company during the past several months has prompted this report, which was prepared at the request of T. G. Mariposa, director of manufacturing. The report has two main purposes:

1. To determine the number and causes of accidents in the factory during the past six months, the responsibility for them, the extent of injuries incurred, and the cost to the company.

2. Based on the findings in number 1 above and on a thorough study of successful safety programs in other companies, to make recommendations for changes in safety rules, procedures, and administration at Crown Manufacturing Company.

Pages 156-157

TRAINING PROGRAMS

Personalized safety training most effective:

1. Can consider individual differences of employee.

2. Permits consideration of worker's learning rate, interests, natural ability, and physical limitations.

3. Can be specific (group training must be general).

Key to successful job-safety training is telling employee what the hazards are and how to avoid them.

Conover, Safety in Industry,
McGraw-Hill, 1980

Page 173

Authorities agree on these six main leadership duties and responsibilities of district supervisors:

1. Interpret company policies as they affect employees and the general public.

2. Maintain an adequate district sales force, backed by a capable, properly motivated office staff.

3. Conduct continual on-the-job training programs for all salespeople.

4. Review the job performance of each representative and supervisor at least once a year with a view toward productive personalized training to overcome individual weaknesses.

5. Make sure the district office has the best possible salespeople that careful recruiting, training, and supervision can provide.

6. Improve the company's image as it appears to employees and the general public.

Page 177

Dear T. R.:

It was great seeing you in Minneapolis in April. Your job with Carson Electronics sounds wonderful, and I congratulate you again on reaching the lofty position of new product development manager.

You may remember our discussion of the Giant Lilliput desk computer. I am very much interested in this computer; from your description I'm encouraged to think it might be the answer to some of our communications problems. So be sure to send me whatever literature you have on it.

Did you know that Ken Breedlove has taken a job with Zellerbach in Houston? Assistant advertising manager, I believe.

Sincerely,

Pages 179

Dear Miss Brennan:

You're right—your account is paid in full. Our statement was mailed before we received your check for $64.88.

Thank you for writing. I hope you have a very successful fall season.

Cordially yours,

Page 181

1. Just as soon as we receive your color preferences on the modular office units, we will make shipment at once.

2. The contracts will be mailed before the end of next week.

3. If in the future you will send your order to my attention, I will see that it is promptly handled.

4. I have taken the liberty of sending you Model 3K instead of Model 4B, which has been discontinued. The price is the same, and I think you might even be happier with the substitution.

5. I'm pleased to say that the strike is now over and we can ship on December 3. I hope this will be in plenty of time for your Christmas promotion.

Page 183

Dear Miss Wigent:

I appreciate your writing me about purchasing an advertisement in The Chieftan.

I am sure you will understand, Miss Wigent, that it would not be possible for us to advertise in all the thousands of yearbooks published each year, even though we'd like to. And so that we show no favoritism, we have established the policy of purchasing yearbook advertising only in the Grand Rapids area where we are located. That makes sense to us: local business support for local community projects.

I hope you will be able to sell your space to the business organizations in and around Lakeville. Good luck!

Sincerely yours,

Page 184

Dear _____ :

Although our name sounds like an educational institution, we are actually a business firm serving as design consultants to organizations in the Chicago area.

There are several local institutions that offer courses in design, including Northwestern University (Evanston), the University of Illinois, and the University of Chicago. One private school from which we obtain employees is Crescent School of Design. It is located at 39 South Wabash Avenue (ZIP 60603).

Good luck!

Yours very sincerely,

Index

About the author

Roy W. Poe has taught communications in secondary schools, colleges, university extension classes, and in management development programs. He has been a government training supervisor, an associate dean of a collegiate school of business, and president of a small college. For over twenty years he was a publishing executive, specializing in business books, for one of the country's largest publishers. The author of several business textbooks, Mr. Poe is now a business education consultant and is currently compiling a communications handbook for business executives.